always
next year

always
next year

The 1998-99 season
according to *When Saturday Comes*

BOOKS

First published in 1999 by WSC Books Ltd
3 Luke Street, London EC2A 4PX

©WSC Books 1999

ISBN 1 897850 48 4

Printed in the UK by Thruxton Press, Andover

Edited by Andy Lyons and Mike Ticher
Design by Doug Cheeseman
Cover illustration by Mick Marston
Thanks to Richard Guy

contents

introduction

Pick up any standard football history in years to come and you will almost certainly find that the 1998-99 season was the crowning glory of Alex Ferguson's era at Manchester United. You probably won't have to read far before you get to words such as "unprecedented", "Treble" and "injury time".

You may find those words in this collection too, though they won't necessarily refer to the same events. As ever, most fans' attention was focused primarily on the trials of their club, whether it was in the Premiership or the Conference, and we have attempted to include reflections on the season at all levels.

Yet United's triumph was entirely appropriate as a symbol of the shifting values and priorities of modern football. The club's subsequent decision to pull out of the FA Cup and its well-publicised tour of China and Australia in the close season showed all too glaringly where the road leads for those clubs which are now plcs and are committed to becoming a global brand.

It is not only clubs the size of United who have to pay attention to what is going on outside their domestic league. The emergence of the Champions League has had a profound impact on fooball in smaller

European countries, where the leading clubs are caught between aping their richer neighbours (as in Switzerland) or risking total exclusion (as in Northern Ireland).

Even in the lower divisions of England, the concept of the "Bosman free" has opened up a whole new world of cultural exchanges which, as the example of Scunthorpe shows, can lead to unlikely but successful liaisons. At the same time, the globalisation of the transfer market and of TV coverage means that what happens in England cannot be ignored even in leagues as far away as Argentina, Japan and Australia.

So the contributions reflect not only a broad variety of experiences from Britain and abroad, but also a consistent sense of how quickly the game is changing. For some fans the frantic boom years have led to their interest in football being rekindled, while for others they have brought on a mood of profound disillusion.

While our parents and grandparents expected to follow their team in much the same way throughout their lives, no one can predict what being a fan will be like when the generation that grew up in the 1970s gets old. Whether it is the increasing financial demands on Premiership fans, the unchecked influx of foreign players or the type of cars driven by Stockport County players, it seems certain that in future nothing will be quite the same as it was even one year previously.

There will always be a next year. But we cannot even be sure when it will begin (February, if Sepp Blatter gets his way), which tournaments will still be on the fixture list or which clubs will deign to enter them. There's only just time to look back on 1998-99 with a clear eye before it becomes ripe for nostalgia.

Andy Lyons and Mike Ticher

old yorke
new yorke

david wangerin

Aston Villa's striker went to Manchester United for £12.6 million and, for some, another slice of football's old appeal went with him

The dawn of a new season. Hope springs eternal. Everyone is level, nothing has gone wrong, and you are bang on course for the championship. Even the weather is sunny. At the beginning of August, it is always still your year.

At Aston Villa, though, August 1998 feels ominous, foreboding, and more than a little frustrating. It shouldn't be that way, particularly when only a few months earlier nobody wanted the season to end. Since the arrival of John Gregory in February, the upturn in our fortunes had been pronounced. Nine wins in the last 11 league games hurled us from lower mid-table obscurity into Europe. Now there is talk of being dark horses for the championship, talk which admittedly resurfaces whenever we finish in the top ten, but encouraging talk all the same.

But now there is other talk to be wary of, talk from a man who, by the very nature of his position, makes you sit up and take notice, however much you might not want to. And his words are a red rag to a bull, an

Officially Licensed Red Rag, bearing an Umbro logo and a £49.95 price tag.

"We usually get the people we want," Alex Ferguson has been quoted as saying, "and we're very interested in Dwight Yorke."

Oh shit.

Why Dwight? Why him? Why now? Why not Chris Sutton, or Darren Huckerby, or some Spanish or Italian guy? Why United? Why is it our team Ferguson has to mess up?

Anxious fans seek comfort in the words of their chairman. "It's hardly necessary for me to explain to Villa fans what I think of Dwight Yorke," says Doug Ellis. "He's been like a son to me." And this may be the truth. But perhaps that's why we're worried, because sooner or later sons grow up and move out, into a life of their own. Given that Yorke is 27, that time may have come.

Or has it? Eight years as an English footballer have honed his professionalism, that well-rehearsed ability to say next to nothing in the presence of a microphone. When Fergie wants you, it must be hard to purse your lips, but he does. And we keep the faith. He won't go. He likes it here. He could never be one of Them. And besides, we wouldn't let it happen. Faith, though, flies in the face of rumour, speculation and even blind logic. Aston Villa or Manchester United. Well, which would you choose?

The season kicks off with Yorke still in our colours, but only just. Villa are away to Everton and, as tends to happen in these circumstances, the match is almost of secondary importance to the story everyone is poised to write. It ends without a goal. Villa are poor, Everton not much better. More to the point is Yorke's performance, almost universally acknowledged as abject.

United have upped their offer to £10 million – almost twice as much as Villa have ever received for anybody. It's been turned down. And Dwight can bite his lip no longer. "I want to go to Manchester United. The Champions League deadline is on Thursday and I want to be there by then."

Two days later, he is gone.

Football, they say, is a Funny Old Game, supposedly littered with strange twists of fate and bewildering unpredictability. Yet much of it is certain: Italian clubs doing well in Europe, plastic seats spelling this or that across the new stand, TV money triumphing over sporting integrity. Now, Villa fans were being reminded of another inevitability: the one guy in your team who is something really special sooner or later moves to a bigger club. However inevitable it may be, it still comes as quite a shock when you want to believe there aren't any clubs bigger than your own.

An anguished Gregory faces the music. "I realised he was simply not committed to Villa like the other ten players," he says, reflecting on the Everton debacle, "so I took the decision to sell him. And now I must suffer the consequences." He is palpably bitter about Yorke's farewell performance: "If he'd have continued to play like that for the next two years, he would have been going to Aldershot instead of Old Trafford."

"This thing has been going on since last September," laments Ellis, before launching into the declaration all Villa-land has been waiting to hear: "United were the last club I wanted any of our players to go to." Alas, the milk is spilt, and a once fruitful relationship comes to the sort of rancorous conclusion you would expect to find in a divorce court.

We bring you into the big leagues, the Holte End adopts you as their idol, and this is the thanks we get? Manchester Bloody United? Well fuck off then, and don't come back. And you know what? You were never any good in bed, either...

We wouldn't have begrudged him going to Juventus or Real Madrid – or Fenerbahce or Viking Stavanger come to that. When David Platt left for Italy, we had little problem in accepting his departure. Serie A was the place to be seen, and we had nothing against Bari. Old Trafford, though, was another matter. This was The Enemy, the club that not only fills the newspapers and the chain stores, but perpetually stands guard over any trophy worth winning.

And so, for some of us, Dwight Yorke played his last football match on August 15th, 1998. We don't really want to know what happens after that. The sight of him in a Sharp suit is too agonising a reminder of his pedigree, and why it took a £12.6 million transfer to the Club of Clubs for everyone else to recognise it. Other teams further down the food chain may be resigned to such body-blows, but for Aston Villa it is a generous slice of humble pie, and a reminder of the league-within-a-league to which they are denied entry.

Anyone who knows how to hold a pencil could write the rest of the story. Bigger and better things were less than a season away for our hero. He'd be seen in dinner jackets at posh London hotels, and be named to all kinds of fantasy teams. He'd whack in those Beckham crosses as if he'd been doing it all his life, play Fred Astaire to Andy Cole's Ginger Rogers. His face would be all over the news stands, his jersey for sale up and down the high street. And he would lift some very big trophies. Just another footballing inevitability. But it doesn't mean you have to like it, or even accept it.

You do your best to ignore but, given the identity of his new club, drips of information still keep leaking through. It's almost impossible to avoid discovering his goal tally for the season, or in what minute he scored last night. But at least you can skip the papers and *Match of the Day* when you know the torment that awaits, and try to filter out the office conversation when it swings round to how much better a player he is now that he's moved north. You can even refer to him in the past tense.

I'm probably too long in the tooth for heroes, and in any case I'd rather not look upon Yorke as one of them. I was 22 when I saw my first English football match, far too late for a chance to worship Andy Lochhead from the Holte End or scrawl Chico Hamilton's name on my school notebooks. My Villa days have not provided all that many opportunities to watch players who could seriously be described as great. Maybe Peter Withe, in a cultish sort of way, and probably Paul McGrath.

Dwight, though, approached greatness from an angle entirely his own. For a club whose heroes – Dennis Mortimer, Charlie Aitken –

seem renowned mainly for work-rate and the sensible option, a touch of flair goes a long way. And whatever you say about Yorke, he was never short of flair. When the ball came to him, you couldn't afford to look the other way. A back-heel, a step-over, a scissors-kick – for a moment you forgot how much everybody was being paid, how little chance your team had of winning anything and even how much it had cost you to get in.

He probably wasn't the finest player Villa have ever produced – not that I have any idea who is. Maybe he wouldn't even feature in the Dream XI. But good grief, he had style – a style that doesn't feature in the legend the way it might do at Old Trafford or Anfield. His repertoire of spin-moves and shoulder-swivels, the graceful way he glided across the pitch – here was evidence that it really was a beautiful game, even on filthy Saturdays in Birmingham.

What set him apart though, as far as I was concerned, was that famous smile. You could pick it out from anywhere in the ground. He was happy – not "happy-go-lucky" in any stereotypical sense, but happy in the sense of genuinely enjoying what he did.

Graham Taylor had found him, Jo Venglos had given him his senior debut and then came Ron Atkinson, who seemed content to retain him as a squad player. Maybe Yorke's body language was too different from most of the rest of the old pros Big Ron had brought in. And so he was shunted behind the likes of Dalian and Deano, and even Frank McAvennie once or twice. The curse of youth and inexperience was too much for him to overcome. He got kicked, and pushed off the ball, and his confidence suffered. You started to think that maybe he wouldn't be around for much longer, Didier Six revisited: too refined for rugged old England. At the time, the spring of 1994, nobody seemed that bothered.

We had won our first trophy in over a decade without too much of his help. Dalian shinned in the first goal against Manchester United in the Coca-Cola Cup final at Wembley and Deano scored the second and third in a 3-1 win. Why play with anyone else up front? Dwight had been given a run-out in the early rounds, but when it started to get serious he couldn't even find space on the bench. Three goals in his only two starts that season suggests he deserved better.

More playing time came his way the following season, but it was still fortunate that the wheels should start to fall off our classic car of a team when they did. When Big Ron was shown the door and his successor ushered in, the smile on the No 18's face ought to have filled the Holte End. If anybody could recognise the talent of this kid, it was surely the guy who had it in spades when he graced that pitch. To most Villa fans, Brian Little was flair incarnate. Yorke quickly took centre stage and the team started to care again. I'd like to think the two events are not unrelated.

By the start of 1996, he'd caught fire. He scored with dizzying regularity, collar upturned, shirt outside shorts, a new found swagger to his game. He'd stopped getting pushed off the ball and learned how to win free-kicks. He took cheeky penalties, even against David Seaman. He was smarter, stronger. And the smile had never been wider. Didier who?

A month later we won the Coke again, and this time he was in the thick of it. He deserved to be, deserved to ice the cake with that 89th-minute roof-slammer, deserved to parade the pot around Wembley. Of all the reasons we had to be cheerful – FA Cup semi-finalists for the first time in 36 years, terrace idol for a manager, even a half-decent playing strip – perhaps most gratifying of all was proprietorship of a player who was the envy of the league.

It is, of course, a double-edged sword. They said Serie A teams were keeping tabs on him. So were the mega-clubs of the Premiership. "Unsettled" they call it. We all were. Could he really be up for sale? Surely not. Aston Villa didn't so much sell players as got rid of them to make way for better ones. And where was there a better player than Dwight?

Long before Alex Ferguson's overtures or Fleet Street's musings, the relationship between Yorke and the fans had started to sour. But unsettled had taken a long time. Eight years at one club represents something of an era in the game these days. I think of the players we had when he arrived – Nigel Callaghan, Derek Mountfield, Ian Olney – and they're gone, long gone, so gone that they almost belong to a different generation. Era indeed. Would that we witness an era like that again.

The last time I went to see Yorke, I despaired. He fluffed a penalty and seemed content to drift along on the periphery of the game. Most telling of all, the smile had disappeared. It was too serious now. He hung around for another season or so, and knocked in his fair share of goals, but something had changed. He had outgrown us.

We survived his departure. All right, we did a little better than survive. For a while, it felt like we were on course to stuff it up Fergie and Yorkie and the rest of the league as well. Then I turned up for the Fulham Cup tie and spoiled it all. Mid-season capitulation or no, it was still a solid campaign, more solid than most expected. Paul Merson supplied the odd moments of flair. Julian Joachim was very fast, Dion Dublin very tall, and Stan Collymore whatever he was. But none of them was Dwight Yorke.

It's depressing, sure, particularly when you think your team is on the verge of something big, as Villa fans often do. But even more depressing is the thought that no matter how good your club might be, or how much money they throw at someone to try to keep him, they're just not on the same footing as United in the fairytale department. Boys in the Caribbean who dream of the Premiership don't wear claret-and-blue shirts, but I suspect more than a fair few own red-and-white ones. Regardless of who the young Yorke's favourite English football team might have been, I can't help but think that was what ultimately did us in.

Predictably, some fans chose to read more into it – we weren't ambitious enough, we didn't make him the right offer, Ferguson poached him and ought to be shot. They might be right. But many of us suspected that once a link had been established between Yorke and Old Trafford, there might be more to it than just money and the Millionaires' League – the fairytale stuff, the boyhood fantasies that improved wage offers won't change. What proportion of the league fancies You Know Who as the club they'd most like to play for? After all, boyhood fantasies are not confined to the Lesser Antilles. And not that many are given a chance to realise them.

Fans, of course, work to their own agenda. Yorke was a traitor, and traitors are not welcomed back. Come the visit of the Red Devils in December, he was unequivocally *persona non grata*. On the radio, you could pick out whenever he touched the ball. It was embarrassing, but hardly surprising: 15 years after my first visit, I still haven't figured out why they boo the team off the pitch at half-time only to cheer them on their return.

I suspect they've forgotten most of the eight years. They were, lest we forget, a fair few more years than Platt, or Saunders, or their beloved Cascarino ever spent at our place – years when sometimes we were as likely to lose as win, not score as score, battle against the drop as compete for Europe.

And, on reflection, this is probably what endears me so to Dwight Yorke. He was the one remaining link to the Aston Villa I knew and loved, the Aston Villa without giant video screens or megastores or rock anthems – the Aston Villa that was just an English football club rather than aspiring to be a global big-time marketing enterprise. The more I think about it, the more I realise fate couldn't have chosen a more appropriate figure to score the last two goals in front of the old Holte End. Those days are gone, of course – as gone as he is, and equally as unlikely to return. I know – my problem, not his.

Hero, throwback or whatever, the honourable thing would be to wish the guy well, and hope that he lifts enough trophies over the next couple of years to frighten his osteopath. But that's not how it works, is it? You go to your grave bitter that he didn't hang around for just one more year, or maybe two, and take us to the championship, or at least the FA Cup final (please God, just once before I die). There's still a big part of you that wants him to fail miserably, to finish out his career in obscurity, kicking himself for ever leaving us. As if.

For a professional footballer, there is no looking back. Not many ever come to regret a move to Old Trafford – not even Dion Dublin,

I'll bet – and Yorke's first season there has already brought him more glory than all his time at Villa Park. I don't know whether he still brings his bag of tricks to each match, or even whether that grin still lights up the winter months the way it used to. But I really don't want to know any more. May God rest his soul.

distant glens

davy millar

As usual, European football came early in the season to Belfast – and left again shortly afterwards

It's still early August but, as summer paid merely a fleeting visit this year, the streets of east Belfast are witnessing the sort of weather normally associated with a typical October afternoon. It's enough to make you question, yet again, the sanity of those who persist in trying to import the street cafe culture prevalent in more sophisticated, or at least more southerly, parts of Europe.

The only thing to be said in favour of the unseasonal weather is that it provides a more authentic backdrop to tonight's Cup-Winners Cup tie between Glentoran and Maccabi Haifa – hazy evening sunshine brings to mind meaningless pre-season friendlies rather than anything more competitive.

Sadly, Mother Nature seems to be the only one up for the occasion. A combination of post-World Cup fatigue (it's less than a month since Brazil's capitulation in Paris) and years of non-achievement by local clubs on the European stage have left expectation levels stuck pretty much at zero. Neither of tonight's teams appears to have a hope in hell of getting close to the final (although Haifa implausibly go on to beat Paris St-Germain and reach the quarter-finals) and so the crowd is made up of a couple of thousand die-hards, many of whom would have turned up to watch the Glens take on their own reserves.

The sparse attendance means pre-match tension is absent from the terraces – people are wandering about, chatting to friends about anything but the game they're supposedly here to see. It takes the emergence of the two sides to remind everyone what they're here for.

According to cliche the first aim away sides has is to silence the home crowd, to deprive their opponents of the lift that a passionate support can provide. In that case, Haifa must be pretty pleased with themselves after only a few minutes of play. By that stage, they've taken control of the game without doing anything spectacular, or even anything particularly interesting. They're just faster and more determined than Glentoran, leaving nobody in any doubt as to which side is the well-drilled professionals and which is the bunch of part-timers just back from their holidays.

The Glens aren't helping themselves by an ultra-cautious start which treats the half-way line as an insurmountable barrier. Faced with the prospect of an evening watching their side making aimless clearances, the crowd allow themselves a brief display of anger before drifting into a state of slightly irritable boredom.

The match is turning into one of those persistently dull aches which refuses to go away, painful enough to notice but not serious enough to merit treatment. Glentoran aren't attacking and, for all their possession, Maccabi haven't created much. The supporters, deprived of even a defensive crisis to lift them from their torpor, resume their pre-match discussions. Holiday exploits get another airing, last night's TV is dissected and a father's affair with next door's daughter provides evidence that *The Jerry Springer Show* has a dedicated fan-base in Belfast.

The real die-hards in the crowd are getting annoyed with the dilet-tantes who'd lost interest in the game while the optimists and the realists are too busy pouring scorn on each other's view of the Glens' tactical approach to pay much attention to what is actually happening on the pitch. Every so often, another small group ambles off in the direction of the social club or the burger van.

Then a Maccabi striker latches on to a through ball and turns inside his hapless marker before shooting into the bottom corner of the net. It was quick and clean, efficient rather than spectacular, and more than enough to cause a depressed silence to fall all around the crowd. The same thought is etched on to every face – here we go again.

For too long now, the Irish League's annual assault on Europe has resembled one of the traditional marches for which the province is famous. The direction, duration and outcome have become so tiresomely predictable that the entire enterprise has become stripped of all meaning or interest. Each year, three clubs qualify and are drawn against opponents who are based too far east to be glamorous. Each of our representatives falls at this first hurdle with at least one buried by an avalanche of goals.

Already this season (and remember it's less than a month since the end of the previous one) Glentoran have lost their two companions. League champions Cliftonville were destroyed by Kosice of Slovakia, while Omonia Nicosia proved too good for Linfield. Both our clubs were effectively eliminated in the first leg when, on a disastrous July evening, they each lost 5-1.

That was enough to bring on the traditional backlash. Every abortive Euro campaign ends with the Irish League enduring wave upon wave of scorn and ridicule while the local media runs the annual debate about whether our sides should even bother entering. This season, that debate took on an added note of virulence when the *Irish News*, not a paper with a great record of support for the local game, urged readers to turn their backs on the domestic league and instead support Wimbledon's proposed move to Belfast. The anonymous writer seemed to feel that nobody would care if the Irish League disappeared and he surely would have struggled to understand why anybody would bother watching Glentoran play the unknowns af Maccabi Haifa.

Mind you, as half-time arrived, there were some in the crowd who would have seen their point. Here and there, angry expressions prove that somebody still cares but on far too many faces there is a weary indifference. They had come with low expectations and had seen nothing to surprise them. Years of failure at this level had deprived them of hope and left them here, at the end of a long decline, a dwindling bunch of supporters in a run-down stadium watching their side being outclassed by an anonymous bunch of Israelis.

Look around The Oval at the vast swathes of unoccupied terracing and think of all the football fans in Belfast, those oh-so-devoted followers of the game who never bother turning up for a match. They are content to wear their replica shirts with pride, sitting in front of their TVs or the big screens in pubs and clubs as they cheer on their favourite English sides. Some may still profess an allegiance to a local side but all are equally likely to join in the ridiculing of the Irish League.

From the moral high ground of their armchair, they feel justified in feeling superior to those strange individuals who actually go to a local ground to cheer on men playing football instead of watching inch-high figures on a screen. They mock the ability of the players, express derision at the small crowds and consider the run-down stadia both depressing and hilarious. They all hold an opinion on Ronaldo's display against France but none can name more than a couple of Irish League players.

Think bitter thoughts about them and about certain local media personalities, not to mention the *Irish News* writer. In England, those people would have leaped on the football bandwagon, suddenly reinventing themselves as life-long supporters of some famous club or other, full of made-up stories about their early days on the terraces. Away from public view, they'd be desperately chasing up supporters with tales to tell so that they could race back to the office and cobble together an article about a cult figure from the Seventies as proof of their devotion to the game. Here, however, they don't have to pretend. There's no benefit to their career in posing as a fan of a local club. Instead, they'll use that football bandwagon to contrast the fortunes of Man Utd with the local clubs, inevitably finding our clubs wanting and therefore deserving of further ridicule.

No matter how slowly they skimmed through *Fever Pitch*, they didn't get to grips with what supporting a team is all about, how it is entirely possible to get as much from cheering on St Albans as from following the Arse. They don't even know that local sides have had their moments of glory in Europe and refuse to believe that both Glentoran and Linfield have reached quarter-finals at this level. Their trendy irony and cynicism would have been sadly out of place in those days when full houses roared on our part-timers to remarkable feats, when Linfield beat Man City 2-1, only to go out on away goals (Cup-Winners Cup 1971), the same rule which Benfica required against Glentoran en route to the 1968 European Cup final. And don't you just know that, if by some miracle those days returned, all those trend-followers would be fondly reminiscing about the times they experienced at Windsor, Solitude or The Oval.

Whether or not everybody in the crowd has been thinking along exactly these lines, something has fired them up for the second-half and the teams re-emerge to a roar of defiance, of rage, of pleading with the Glens to do something. And they do. Half-time was obviously as unpleasant for them as it was for the fans and they're psyched-up. Tackles are made, bad passes are recovered, midfielders are pushing up, full-backs are overlapping and Haifa, under pressure, are starting to panic at their loss of control.

A couple of scrambles in the Israeli box heighten the tension, those tired faces in the crowd are alive again and the noise level slips up a notch or two. Glentoran attack again, the ball swings into the penalty area and, from among a throng of players, a Glentoran hand rises to direct the ball into the top corner. Even as the ball hits the net you can tell there is something wrong. Some players aren't reacting to the goal and the roar from the crowd has a catch in it, a question mark amid the jubilation. The referee has one arm raised and, no matter how hard the crowd pray it's a penalty, it is, of course, a free-kick to Haifa.

The scare stiffens Israeli resolve and, without regaining the control they enjoyed during the first-half, they pass the crucial 75-minute mark in relative safety. The crowd know from bitter experience that by now the local team is merely hanging on and the atmosphere steadily diminishes. The relative fitness levels mean that Haifa are comfortable while the Glens are engaged in a lung-bursting effort to stay competitive. All the home side can do now is throw bodies in the way, lunge into tackles hoping they don't arrive late enough to get a red card. At this point a top-class side would cash in with another goal or two but Maccabi just aren't good enough.

The crowd is drifting away in a sad and largely silent retreat while the shouts of the players echo around The Oval. The final whistle provokes a round of applause, recognition of the effort put in by the Glens, but it's clear that everybody knows this tie is as good as over. As the last player leaves the pitch, the ground is already almost deserted.

No so long ago, a home defeat by the Israeli cup-holders would have been seen as a bad result, a major let-down for the club, its fans and the local game in general. The years of failure have reduced expectations to such an extent that tonight nobody seems very upset about it at all. It's almost as if this wasn't really a competitive game, an attitude which speaks volumes about what even the most dedicated local fans now expect from their teams.

Glentoran reached a Cup-Winners Cup quarter-final in 1974 but even then ambitions did not extend to actually winning the thing. Now it seems that they, and all the other Northern Irish sides, are scarcely expected to put up even a decent first-round performance. European matches are treated as glorified friendlies, while the only real competitive football takes place within the Irish League. English and Scottish clubs are our flag-bearers in Europe now, the likes of Glentoran are only being given a first-round match as a sort of reward for being good boys during the previous season. The annual debate over whether they should compete in Europe is becoming irrelevant as our sides, and their supporters, have already mentally withdrawn.

Any why not? It's a nice, cosy world inside your very own league. Why disturb that comfortable existence by venturing outside and testing your ability against other people, especially those who take the game more seriously than yourselves? The sort of people who do understand things like training properly, not just spending two nights a week trying to shake off the boredom of the day job. The type of people who don't use the ridiculously early start to their new season as an excuse for their performance but who instead accept the inconvenient timing and prepare for it.

The answer, if any were needed, lay in tonight's attendance. A small crowd which tried hard but was unable to shake off its belief that this match was not really a competitive one. They knew their team hadn't stepped up preparations from all the other European failures and, when your team shows this lack of ambition, you can't be blamed for taking the same approach. Meanwhile, those who stayed away were given yet another reason to turn their backs on local sides in favour of one of the English giants.

This was the last ECWC tie to be played in Belfast and it's sad that the competition went out with such a whimper. The whole evening was far removed from UEFA's preferred image of big-time European football, which is one reason why clubs like Glentoran are squeezed in at the start of the season, sadly cordoned off from bigger, richer sides. One can only hope that the club won't meet the fate of the ECWC itself, unceremoniously dropped to facilitate the greedy ambition of the glamorous few, ending up in a competition restricted to the poor, the obscure and the unwanted.

changing gear

dave espley

A startling truth about modern football was laid bare for all to see in the car parks of Stockport

It was my dad who first disillusioned me. It was teatime in the mid-Seventies, and I was watching *The Tomorrow People*. He arrived home from work, came into the living room and, after a few inconsequential pleasantries, dropped the bombshell.

"I've just seen Johnny Griffiths in Mersey Square."

Johnny Griffiths? Stockport County's blond superstar? Scorer of a fantastic 13 goals in season 1972-73? The man who personified all that was glamorous about Seventies football to my pre-pubescent eyes? Must affect nonchalance.

"Yeah? What was he doing?" Casing the centre of Stockport for a site for his new boutique? Cutting the ribbon of the new Tesco? Just casually loafing around, signing the odd autograph?

"Waiting for a 17 to Reddish."

The shattering of childhood illusions is a uniquely painful experience. Footballers don't catch buses. Even if both their Jags are being serviced, they've got chauffeurs to drive them around. They don't live in bloody Reddish, either – they've got purpose-built futuristic houses just outside Bramhall with tellies that come out of the walls when you press a button (George Best had a lot to answer for). They're footballers, for God's sake!

I'm not sure I was entirely convinced he wasn't pulling my leg for years afterwards. Not, that is, until I became a County scratchcard seller and thus achieved access to the inner sanctum of the club (which turned out to be a series of grimy corridors). I gradually realised from close observation that County players were just young men like any others, and not especially well paid young men at that. The spectacle of players arriving on foot with their boots in a plastic bag was not an uncommon one.

Indeed, there was one particular story, which had a definite ring of truth, concerning the team captain helping out behind the bar of a local pub until late on the night before a crucial Cup game. (The word "crucial" is relative here. It was a first round tie away at Caernarfon Town but it turned out to be pretty bloody crucial to us – we lost.) County players, whatever was the case at the big Manchester two, were ragged-arsed plebs like the rest of us. Thus, over the years, was the pain of my dad's innocently delivered revelation dulled.

Imagine my distress, then, halfway through last season, when my perspective was shaken for a second time. It wasn't a particularly memorable footballing year, not when we'd had promotion and a League Cup semi-final two short years before. We consolidated our position in the First Division and, although we didn't maintain the momentum that saw us finish in our highest ever position the previous season (eighth), we were never in serious danger of relegation. In truth, a good deal of the football was dire, culminating in a 5-0 loss to relegated Oxford on the final day. But if on-field events were unremarkable, there was at least one major shock off the pitch for me.

Walking to Edgeley Park one day to collect tickets for some game or other (it really was that sort of season) I was surprised to see a number of shiny, expensive cars parked outside. Here a Porsche Boxster, there a BMW convertible, everywhere a 4x4. My first thought was that the new restaurant the club had built was hosting some kind of flash gits conference – computer sales reps, perhaps – but it was only when I saw the registration plate of the soft-top BMW that the penny dropped. M10 KYF. Micky F. Mike Flynn. Team captain. Christ, these are the players' cars!

Having one's footballing illusions shattered twice in one lifetime is not an experience I would greatly recommend. Of course, I knew that following our recent success (and the 33 per cent increase in admission prices that the, ahem, glamour of First Division football brought with it) there was clearly a lot more money sloshing around at Edgeley Park, even if our total turnover would probably not even match that of the smaller of the two footballing superstores down the road at Old Trafford.

I'd clocked the column that Carlo Nash wrote in the programme – called "Carlo's Cars" natch – in which the *Top Gear*-fixated goalkeeper waxed lyrical about the imminent arrival of his flash new motor, with hardly a raised eyebrow. But actually seeing the vehicular wealth so ostentatiously displayed in the car park really hit home. Even if the top five cars on show would have had David Beckham turning his nose up – and let's be honest, his garage is probably bigger than County's car park – the fact is that, by any normal measure of affluence, Stockport County footballers are now wealthy.

It's a sobering thought. For all last season's talk that we were now a better team than Manchester City (and there was a lot of that, believe me), we know our place. We are a little club living above our station. We might, with a bit of luck, become established in the First Division and become a medium sized club living, while not quite above our station, still camped out on the roof of the Burger King on platform one. We might even, with a bit of luck and a following wind, become a medium-sized club with a Barnsleyesque tilt at the Premiership for a year. But we are not, and never will be, a "big club". Yet our players drive new BMWs with personalised registrations.

The "big-money-in-the-Premiership-these-days" story is almost as boring as the "Was-Giggs's-goal-the-best-ever?" debate. Talk of players earning £20,000 a week, or even £1 million as a signing-on fee, have become commonplace. But what is, to my mind, remarkable, is that there is a form of trickle-down economics at work in football today – and even the PFA have recognised this phenomenon.

I recently caught a glimpse of their glossy house magazine. It's an interesting read, or at least the adverts are. Assuming a generous average of 25 professionals earning silly money at each of the 20 Premiership clubs, there may be a total of around 500 in the mega-rich zone. It's clear that such a magazine would not survive on such a tiny readership. More to the point, Posh Pavings or Flash Homes Abroad would not shell out for their glossy display advertisements if they thought their market was so limited. Clearly, the magazine is aimed at the whole of the PFA membership, from Premiership to Third Division.

When average players (we've only got two or three at Stockport who could in any way be described as above average, and there were a lot of flash cars in that car park) at a farty little club like County can command salaries that would cause even the chairmen of the priva-tised utilities to blush coquettishly, it really does make you pause for thought.

Okay, then, pause for thought. Footballers in general – and County players in particular – are now wealthy. Does it matter? As a fan whose first 17 years supporting the club were spent watching a constant diet of generally abysmal Fourth Division tripe, surely I can't complain about the footballing caviar that's been served up in the last decade? For while 1998-99 was not a memorable season, it was still a season of consolidation in the First Division.

In the days when Johnny Griffiths was County's glamour boy, we were firmly rooted at the foot of the Fourth Division, and the division we're in now, if it impinged on our football consciousness at all, was merely the place where the nearly-big clubs lived. For County to have established themselves at that level is surely a cause for unalloyed celebration.

We've all heard the tales of the maximum wage days. How, travelling on the top deck of the bus, fans would turn round to cadge a fag from the bloke behind them, only to find themselves addressing one of the players – who would probably be able to supply the fag as well. No one could seriously desire a return to those days, not least because players were treated as little more than serfs by chairmen who were never required to state, in the days when players' wages were capped, where exactly the revenue from those record attendances went. However, many would maintain that the pendulum has swung too far the other way.

Despite our high-earning players, average crowds at Edgeley Park are still only hovering around the 7,000 mark, meaning that the club has had to rely, to an ever-increasing extent, on the commercial department to pay those wages. In purely financial terms, the club is proving a remarkable success. The aforementioned restaurant is part of the marketing strategy for the huge Cheadle End that was built a couple of seasons ago, and if such things have a distinct "bolted on afterwards" air – as though the club looked at the cavernous spaces under the seats and thought "Mmm, we really should do something there, you know" – then the next stage in the development of Edgeley Park is genuinely staggering for fans like me, who remember the days of players catching buses.

Plans were announced towards the end of the season for an identical stand to the Cheadle End for the opposite end of the ground, to be completed in the summer of 2000, thus completing the transition to all-seater status. The difference in the price of the two developments, however, from £1.5 million to around £10 million, is not merely explained by inflation. No, the reason for the increase is more to do with the fact that behind the stand a hotel is planned which will almost rival those at Old Trafford and Stamford Bridge.

A recent business development paper bemoaned the lack of decent hotel facilities in Stockport as the one thing that was holding the town back (in business development terms, that is) and, to give them credit, the County board have seized upon this in an attempt to persuade the council to grant planning permission and possibly financial support to develop the hotel. It can be fairly confidently assumed that the project will be a feasible profit-making venture – there will be a lot of private money tied up in that £10 million and private money tends not to speculate too wildly when bill reaches eight figures.

I have referred to events on the pitch last season as "wholly unremarkable" but if I'm honest "wholly crap" would be a fairer description. Most of the football was dire, culminating in a 5-0 defeat by relegated Oxford on the last day. Yet crucial to the success of the hotel scheme, we are told by the board, is that County must remain a First Division club.

Presumably because the board thought, after such a poor season, that Gary Megson might jeopardise that aim, he was sacked at the end of June, ostensibly because he applied for other jobs while still employed by County. It was a laughable excuse – how many of us would remain in work if that was a sackable offence? In reality, many suspect he paid the price for the commercial shenanigans that are just as important – more so, in the minds of the suits – as what happens on the pitch these days, even at clubs like County.

In some ways, Megson's dismissal reinforced the feelings of unreality I experienced when I saw the cars in the car park that day. In the days of Johnny Griffiths, any County manager who avoided finishing in the bottom four, thus requiring the chairman to call in a few favours at re-election time, would feel pretty chuffed with his exploits. If the team finished in the top half of the Fourth Division (a purely hypothetical speculation), we fans would have picketed the Bells distillery, demanding to know why he hadn't received his due managerial recognition. The club is unrecognisable from the one I started supporting, in so many ways.

I pass George Best's old house on the way to work these days. It has been up for sale recently, at an asking price in the £300,000-£400,000 range. It's a nice looking place, especially since a post-Best owner, presumably not a fan of the "Seventies high tech" school of architecture, got rid of the flat roof and white walls. What I find most remarkable, however, is that as I cycle past and take an affectionate look, I'm suddenly ten years old again. If Johnny Griffiths was playing for County today, he could probably afford to buy it.

firm smack of corruption

ken gall

By the end of the season the dominance of Rangers and Celtic was not just boring, it was also steadily poisoning Scottish football

Anyone seeking a defining image of Scottish football as it enters its third century surely could do no better than the illicitly-shot video footage of the then Rangers vice-chairman Donald Findlay singing "Fuck the Pope", while Neil McCann, Rangers' most prominent – and perhaps only – Scots-born Roman Catholic employee grimaces in the background.

Allied to a Fatboy Slim-style soundtrack, the repeated broadcasting on Sky TV of this remarkable clip would help to send the elemental message of what the Old Firm – and, consequently, Scottish football – are all about: arrogance, limitless self-delusion, over-conspicuous consumption and the undoubted, if subtle, manipulation of some very dubious sympathies within their respective fan bases. The consequences were to be seen on the night after the Cup final.

On the same night as Findlay's now-infamous karaoke session, Thomas McFadden, a 16-year-old Glaswegian wearing a Celtic strip, was stabbed and died from his wounds. He had watched the Cup final on television, because his mother was worried about potential crowd violence at Hampden. Another Celtic fan was hit in the chest by, of all things, a crossbow bolt while walking home from the game. The culture which the Old Firm feeds off – as demonstrated by Findlay – is no longer merely malevolent, it is becoming rotten.

Findlay's subsequent resignation was described, apparently with a straight face, as "honourable" by the head of a Rangers' supporters organisation. However, one might have thought that a summary dismissal from Rangers chairman David Murray, who has pledged to end sectarianism at Ibrox, might have sent a better message.

Indeed, Findlay's resignation letter, in which he used the "serious lapse of judgment" line favoured by Lawrence Dallaglio, Ron Davies and a host of other humble-pie eaters, seemed to imply that it was not what he had done that had resulted in his sad departure, but the fact that he had been caught. One can only wonder at the mentality of Findlay, who sang Orange marching songs to an audience including Latin, eastern European and, of course, Scottish Roman Catholics.

The death of Thomas McFadden, allied to the sheer crassness of Findlay's behaviour – forgetting, for a moment, the mind-numbing mediocrity of the football on display in the Cup final – leads one to ponder how long the Old Firm can continue as they are before fans, players and, most importantly, investors and the media become irrevocably cheesed off with them.

Images from the Old Firm championship decider on May 2nd must have been greeted with dismay by those whose job it is to seek sponsorship and investment for the Scottish game – referee Hugh Dallas lying on the Parkhead turf covered with his own blood, or Vidar Riseth receiving a standing ovation from 60,000 Celtic fans for a waist-high kick at Tony Vidmar. Any hopes that things would not get worse were to be dashed comprehensively on Cup final day.

On the morning of the final, the *Daily Record*, Scotland's main tabloid, called on the fans of both clubs not to let the nation down and to make the first game at the refurbished Hampden a showpiece occasion. (Lovers of perspective will note that the *Record* devoted 16 pages to the game, and a little over 20 paragraphs to the prospect of nuclear war between India and Pakistan. The headline on the latter, **Spectre Of Armageddon Returns**, might have referred to either.)

The *Record*'s front page boasted a posed photograph of Celtic's Dolph Lundgren lookalike (and playalike) Johan Mjallby and the Rangers captain Lorenzo Amoruso in what looked like an advertisement for a gay dateline. The adjoining copy did little to dispel that thought: "They are two talented professionals at the top of their careers... but they are also, as our exclusive picture shows, friends." The events of the following night suggested that pleas for an Old Firm love-in were not taken to heart by everybody.

While the hogwash purloined by the *Record* and much of the rest of the Scottish media suggested the title decider and the Cup final were sporting (and national) occasions of the utmost importance, let there be no doubt that these encounters were sideshows in European football. The real stuff, as ever, was happening elsewhere – in Barcelona, Manchester, Marseille and Milan.

The players on view were, almost to a man, those offloaded or unwanted by the proper clubs in Europe. Henrik Larsson, whose signature on a lucrative contract in March appeared to be his last attempt at physical effort of the season, was not beating off Serie A clubs with a stick when he left Feyenoord. Andrei Kanchelskis, like Gascoigne before him, seems to be having a career in reverse. Gabriel Amato, of whom little was known before his arrival at Ibrox, has been replaced by the even more obscure Michael Mols, from Utrecht.

However, it is in the introduction of local talent that both clubs have failed most visibly. A generation of Scottish players has been denied an opportunity to bid for a place on the biggest domestic stages due to the impatience of the clubs and their fans. Barry Ferguson was a regular starter for Rangers at the start of the season and, heaven help us, actually resembled a proper footballer. However, injury and weariness conspired against him, Charlie Miller and other youngsters of potential who, frustrated by the lack of opportunity at Ibrox, have faded into obscurity; in Miller's case, a loan spell at Leicester.

For their part, Celtic brought Simon Donnelly into the first team some years ago. Blond and baby-faced, Donnelly looked like a player until, alas, he was damned by the description as "the new Dalglish", a term used by the Scottish media about any young Celt who can kick a football without raising a substantial divot. Sadly, Donnelly's inability to become the new King Kenny has been followed by a downward spiral, resulting in his unmourned transfer to Sheffield Wednesday.

Rangers, the club of Morton, Waddell and Baxter, are now little more than a group of anonymous Euro-mercenaries, assembled at ludicrous expense. The £30 million or so that Dick Advocaat spent before the season must be regarded by anyone with a semblance of sanity as grossly excessive when put against the job at hand: winning the Scottish championship. At the end of each season that group is broken up to make way for another set of anonymous mercenaries, assembled at an even more absurd cost.

As for Celtic, their boundless weepy sentimentalism, creeping paranoia and financial, managerial and transfer speculation have gone well beyond the point of tedium. The endless harking back to heroes of the past such as Stein, the Lisbon Lions, Dalglish and even Charlie Nicholas, invariably deflects attention from the sub-standard quality of the present product. They have tried to play Rangers at their own game, with spectacularly unsuccessful results. The obsession of each for the other, particularly while the remaining teams in the Premier League no longer seem capable of coming to terms with them, is stifling Scottish football. More importantly, it leads to tragedies such as the death of Thomas McFadden.

What is to be done with them both? The introduction of more cosmopolitan line-ups, including the almost seamless introduction of Neil McCann at Ibrox, has done nothing to lessen the vitriol unleashed by the fans. Findlay, a man who had sat at the top table at Ibrox for many years and whose sympathies must have been known to David Murray, is only an indicator of the mentalities entrenched in the boardrooms at Ibrox and Parkhead.

As is so often the case in football today, the problems are exacerbated by money. The term "Old Firm" was not dreamed up to indicate any strength of purpose or certainty at Ibrox or Parkhead. Rather, it resulted from the belief in the early years of the century that, where money was concerned, the two clubs would put aside their mutual antipathy in pursuit of the almighty buck. What has changed now?

Some laudable attempts have been made, such as Celtic's Bhoys Against Bigotry campaign, to improve the situation, but Findlay's behaviour, and that of Celtic's fans and players during the title decider, would suggest that the clubs are only paying lip service to a problem that neither wholeheartedly wishes to be solved. After all, Celtic have more than 50,000 season ticket holders, and Rangers' average crowd is not much lower. Do those in charge really wish to lower the tone of antagonism which, in part, motivates so many people to watch what can only be described as second-rate football in Glasgow?

How hard would it be, for example, for David Murray or Celtic's new chief executive Allan MacDonald to take some of the heat out of the situation by banning Union Jacks and Irish tricolours from each stadium, or by ending the playing of what Findlay likes to think of as "folk songs" at both grounds?

In the end, the answer may lie with the paymasters – Sky TV, the Royal Bank of Scotland, Nike, Umbro and the other big firms involved in pumping money into "Scottish football", by which is meant, of course, the Old Firm. The seemingly endless violence and bigotry, and the absolute dearth of quality of the footballing product must, in time, cause them to reassess their financial input.

Perhaps it is asking too much for all concerned to take their eyes off the cash register to try to achieve a small step in sporting and social progress in Scotland for the new century. At present, Rangers and Celtic, their fans, the Scottish media and the Scottish game's financial backers are all participants in an association that is in danger of becoming corrupt in all senses but the financial. The shame of Donald Findlay and the murder of Thomas McFadden made it all too clear.

talking
my language

simon kuper

There are worse ways to make a living than interviewing foreign footballers. One of which is interviewing English footballers

I was lying on the sofa one Sunday afternoon in December (it gets more interesting than this) when the phone rang.

"Hi," said a voice.

"Hi," I replied.

After a while I felt compelled to ask: "Who's this?"

"Guess," said the voice, in a foreign accent.

I made a couple of educated guesses.

"No!" shouted the voice. "It is Boudewijn!"

He was quite right. It was Boudewijn Zenden, winger for Barcelona and Holland, the young stocky one who dribbled past a couple of players and put the ball into the top corner against Croatia in the World Cup third-place play-off. It was the first time a professional footballer had ever telephoned me at home.

I had interviewed Zenden in Barcelona the month before and he was calling to say how much he liked the resulting article. He admired the structure, he said. We then fell into desultory chat. He asked how things were in London. I said he must drop round some time and he said he would love to. Then he said goodbye.

I know I should be blasé about these things. I have been writing about football on and off for years, and spent much of the season travelling and writing a column about foreign football for the *Observer*, but I still think footballers are different from the rest of us. This year I found out that some of them are nice too.

The process of discovery began in Munich in September, when I was waiting rather nervously by the side of 1860 Munich's training pitch for practice to end. I was there to interview Gerald Vanenburg, 1860's Dutch sweeper, but I did not have an appointment. You may remember Vanenburg as the underweight midget with dark, frizzy hair who played for Holland in the 1980s. When he was only 15 he was teaching Ajax first-team players tricks, and in 1982 he perpetrated a legendary outside-of-the-right-foot lob. Had Vanenburg been larger and of greater mental stability he would have been great. As it was, he won about ten league titles, the European Championship with Holland and the European Cup with PSV Eindhoven. He was also one of my childhood heroes.

When training ended and the players came off the pitch, I walked up to him and got as far as the word "Hello" (the same in Dutch as it is in English, incidentally) when he reached out, shook my hand, and said: "Hi. I'm Gerald."

"I know," I said. I asked him for an interview. A look of sorrow crossed his little face. He was unconscionably busy that day, he said. He had just moved to Munich and builders were arriving to redo his house. Still, he could spare me half an hour.

We sat in the beer garden that fronts the training ground and he gabbed away for nearly two hours. Vanenburg was the perfect host. He persuaded me to have a full-scale lunch, advised me to try a certain rather complicated fruit drink that was a house speciality and, when I asked the waitress, dressed in traditional Bavarian costume, for the bill, he held up his hand. "Can you put this on expenses?" he asked.

"Yes," I said. I know he is a multimillionaire, but it was touching even so. I paid, though. A top-class footballer who gives you an interview is providing you with a product worth several hundred pounds. It was not the most exciting interview ever, but one thing Vanenburg said stuck in my mind: "I think that I was a very special player. It's terrible to say it about yourself, but I could and can do everything with a ball. Everything I tried worked. Name me another player who had that too."

He was absolutely right and I admire him more for saying it than if he had told me, "Oh, you know, you just go out there and do your best." Here was a man who understood his gift. What is interesting about great footballers is not their private lives or their relationships with managers but their gift, the thing that makes them different. Some of them can talk about it.

It is the justification for interviewing footballers; that, and the fact that, just as much as our friends, they are characters in our lives whom we want to understand. Marco van Basten refuses interviews, asking, "What do I have to say that makes me more interesting than a carpenter?" A few things, actually.

From Munich I crossed the world to Chicago. On an October evening I found myself in the Chicago Fire locker-room talking to Frank Klopas, an American international who a few minutes before had scored the golden goal that had given the Fire the US Cup. Klopas talked about how proud he was that the Fire had so many American players, how sad he found it that Chelsea had so many foreigners, and then he sprayed champagne over me. For months now I have been trying to imagine the same scene in the Manchester United changing room at Wembley.

In November, a Dutch magazine sent me to Dortmund to ask the German centre back Jürgen Kohler about one subject only: his relationship with Marco van Basten, whom he had marked for Germany and Juventus. It turned out I had stumbled on Kohler's particular obsession. We sat in a hut with a coffee pot next to Borussia Dortmund's training ground and Kohler talked and talked and talked. He told me about a photograph of himself and Van Basten shaking hands after a match. "To me, that says it all," Kohler said, transported. It seemed Kohler, despite winning the World Cup in 1990, was a man with a large inferiority complex who needed to believe he enjoyed Van Basten's esteem. So he told me endless stories about how he and Van Basten had played hard, but had always respected one another.

At the launch of his autobiography, asked by journalists to read out a passage, Kohler had chosen a eulogy that he had solicited, through the friend of a friend, from Van Basten, which said in effect that Kohler was a good player. Personally I would have read the bit about lifting the World Cup, but there you go. The conversation was a bizarre insight into Kohler's psyche. Then he drove off in his Jag.

There was one thing I did not have the heart to mention to Kohler. "Kohler," Van Basten had mused after Holland had beaten Germany in the 1988 European Championship. "Who was that?"

In February, Bruce Grobbelaar was training a Cape Town team called Seven Stars. I went up to him after practice expecting nothing. After all, if you were Bruce Grobbelaar would you talk to a British journalist? Instead he put me in his car and drove me into town. We had several beers, and considerably more the next night, when I collapsed in a drunken stupor in his spare room after he had pondered the serendipity of life over a final whisky chaser on the veranda. (What does Bruce Grobbelaar keep in his spare room? About a dozen hats of various kinds and Nelson Mandela's autobiography.)

Throughout our conversations I was taking down what he said in my notebook, yet he continued to talk in the most open way possible about his private life and ambitions. You would have thought Grobbelaar had learned something from the past few years. In the end, writing up the interview, I cut out a fair deal just to protect him. He was very nice. And there is something special about being driven around Cape Town by Bruce Grobbelaar, even if it is at 100 miles per hour on the inside lane.

I thank God on my bare knees that I only write about foreign football for the *Observer*. I would rather do almost any job than have to chase interviews with English footballers. Journalists who interview David Beckham get their intelligence insulted by his responses. British players suffer for it, too. If they treated journalists better, the journalists might start regarding them as humans. If you know that a player is human, you treat a bad performance with more circumspection.

Watching Zenden in the World Cup semi-final against Brazil, when I already knew him slightly, I felt nervous for him, as you do when watching a friend speak in public. And if a player is a nice guy, you feel that he deserves the adulation. This is a problem in British football: almost everyone recognises that the national heroes are a bunch of dolts. It makes for an uneasy relationship.

As I write, the newspapers are saying that Newcastle and Coventry want Zenden. If he calls again, I'll tell him not to go.

house of cards
simon bell

Former Conference stars Woking were watched by the biggest post-war crowd for an FA Cup qualifying round match. But that was about as good as it got

Call it the seven-year itch, if you like. It's probably a coincidence that Woking's ropiest season since making our bow at the top level of non-League football was our seventh, but it makes for a catchy title. And if it helps a few folk at the club to believe that what occurred in August and September 1998 was some sort of inevitable numerological act of fate, well so be it. It makes as much sense as anything else.

What didn't make sense to anyone was that come ten to five on September 5th, we, Woking FC, FA Cup giant-killers, non-League media darlings and general pot-hunting glory boys, were bottom of the Conference with one point from seven games.

The home game against Barrow was, for many Woking fans, concrete proof that God just didn't like us any more. The concrete in question appeared to have set solid around the ankles of our back four (or three, or five – it was hard to be sure). Henry Moore could have sculpted the lot of them as a group work: Reclining Figures With Gaping Hole, perhaps. The Cumbrians had just become the third team in 14 days to beat us 3-2. Having battled back from 2-0 down only to lose 3-2 in the 97th minute against Southport, we'd gone all experimental and taken two-goal leads against Kidderminster and Barrow, then thrown them away.

There are only so many times you can have a laugh about that sort of thing. Unless, of course, you're John McGovern. With a two-year contract in his pocket, Brian Clough's former bagman could afford to lean against the dugout – the one without the dry-rot, at least – and wait for the board to work their way through the series of arcane rituals that would lead to his departure up the M1 with a safely-trousered contract pay-off, rumoured to be about 70 grand. Like you'd be bothered what people thought of you, wouldn't you?

It's all too easy to accept that he was led to believe things about money that later proved not to be the case (that Conference players don't ask for it, for instance) but when push came to shove he just wasn't very good, really. Thankfully, shove arrived in record time – only three weeks after we'd started baying for it – and despite the fact that the decision to show him the door was not unanimous.

The long slog back to respectability finally began under a manager who knew what he was doing. Sadly, it began without bright prospect Kevin Betsy, sold to Fulham. McGovern's own version of events appears to indicate that Kev was flogged to finance the manager's pay-off. It's probably a good job he moved out of his houseboat on the Basingstoke Canal land-based premises when he did.

Whatever the facts of McGovern's departure, from that point my personal fear eased. It really was fear: nothing as middling as concern or anxiety. Not fear of the mid-term consequences of a poor sequence of results. Not even fear of relegation, as such (I've watched enough Isthmian League football not to be suicidal about the prospect of having to do so again). Rather, it was because the stakes are a lot higher than they used to be for a club like Woking. The longer-term effect of a lousy season is potentially terminal.

In the seven years we've been official Football League wannabes,

Cards have usually finished "thereabouts" in the Conference (although never "there"). Partly on the strength of this, but also very largely because of ex-manager Geoff Chapple's touch in the more glamorous knockout competitions, the club managed to negotiate £1.1 million from the local council towards a nice new stand. Suddenly, at least a quarter of Kingfield looks like those proper grounds you see on the telly. If you shut one eye. We have all the other trappings of a non-League club on the move: a shop with more stock items than staff, some evidence of painting in the bar, a family section sponsored by those noted guardians of our children's future, McDonalds. What we've also got is a wage bill that would float a small country for a year, and no very obvious way of financing it safely.

If you were to mention to the average supporter of any number of non-League clubs that Woking had financial difficulties, they'd laugh. Partly dismissively, partly on the off-chance that it might be true (we're not universally loved). Fact is, despite all the "stockbroker belt" cliches, we're not flush. Nor are we untypical.

This season has seen Hereford, Barrow, Farnborough and Leek, to mention only Conference clubs, discover that the wolf at the door has acquired a set of keys and is stood in the hall, compiling an inventory. Each story is different, and in the case of a couple of clubs the news of organised crime moving into non-League football has added a bizarre twist, but the fact is that it still costs too much to compete at the top end of the non-League game.

After the Barrow match, I sat in the car and did some sums. Nothing to do with anything so trite as points needed to beat the drop, or shots on target. I was working out how long the board could afford not to pay McGovern off with gates 20 per cent below the previous season's average. Nothing could be more bleak. It may very well be about glory and doing things in style, but nowadays fans of smaller clubs are more likely to attend games with calculators than rattles.

That half-time game of Count The Crowd (often brought forward to midway through the first half in McGovern's time, in the name of entertainment) has a new urgency about it. Without any fearsome marketing engine, a club like Woking has few sources of income except bodies through the turnstile. Even the main corporate sponsor probably only accounts for ten per cent of the annual wage bill. And when you consider our board...

Let's not be too hard. We are in the enviable position of having a group of people running the club who actually care about it. Most of them, the chairman Jon Davies included, have been going for over 30 years. But that might just be half the problem. Here we are, three or four good unbeaten runs away from the Football League, and the people in charge appear to have only the haziest notion of what running the business side of a professional football club might consist of. In short, the ambition which has driven the club over the past decade or so has dangerously outstripped its capacity to manage.

Part of this is down to the nature of the Conference. You have 22 clubs, all supposedly there to scrap for a single promotion place, all forced by the competition to pay wages comparable to those in the Third Division while, with the other hand, dragging facilities up to a standard fit to compare with the palaces of our betters. All this on the basic income from gates which average 1,500 or so across the league.

Part of our own problem, though, stems from the particular nature of the club. Woking were always part of the Isthmian League, the historically amateur structure whose clubs were initially excluded from invitation to the Alliance Premier League in 1979 for not being sufficiently professional. Woking, in fact, clung to the notion that paying players to turn out was somehow vulgar long after the rest of the Isthmian had embraced "shamateurism" – clandestine payments to nominal non-pros – with gusto.

The people who run the club, although now the board of a limited company, still give the impression that it's all a bit distasteful. They might be right, but we're not playing Corinthian Casuals any more. We're playing Stevenage, Rushden and several hard-nosed business set-ups who know what football is like at a higher level than ours and what it takes to stay there – for a while at least.

It's not that we can't see the consequences of staying still, or indeed going backwards. This year, for the first time since 1990, we had to qualify for the FA Cup. OK, success has spoiled us. But the truth is we'd forgotten anyone had to do anything that menial. And now that we do, who do we automatically come up against? Aldershot Town. The Shots are most people's idea of a footballing good cause. To the dewy-eyed romantic they symbolise the ultimate price paid by football's struggling poor, and what can be achieved by a group of supporters who are determined to fight back in the face of gross injustice and the depredations of incompetent owners. To us, they're mostly just a pain in the bum.

I wouldn't wish the closure of their club on any group of supporters, but if forced I could make an exception for Aldershot. When it actually happened in 1992, I was equivocal. If that seems callous, you have to understand what it's like to support a club so small that it gets patronised by another club which has flowerbeds at one end of its ground.

Aldershot fans were, or always seemed to me to be, lairy on the most slender of pretexts. Give them something half-worthwhile to celebrate (their Fourth Division play-off win over Wolves in 1988, say) and they become insufferable. I'm sure the feeling's entirely mutual. Even now, seven years after the reformation of Aldershot as "Town" and despite following a club which has achieved things his can only dream about, I half expect my one Shots-supporting friend to ruffle my hair when talk turns to Woking.

This season, the ante was upped by Aldershot's presence in the Ryman Premier, just one league below us. We still only had 13 points from 14 games. They had a couple of ex-Woking players at the back, an ex-Conference journeyman centre-forward in Gary Abbott who will never be on any Woking fan's Christmas card list, and were managed by George Borg, ditto.

George is what I think diplomats would call "eccentric". During one FA Cup game between his old side, Enfield, and Woking, he became so emotionally overwrought that the Enfield physio had to try to restrain him. George took a swing at him. Rumours that George was in the running for the Woking manager's position after Geoff Chapple's departure were widely assumed to have been circulated by the club to ease the passage of the potentially unacceptable McGovern. They'd have eased the passage of Pol Pot.

The match itself was mentioned in a few national papers. One took the angle that it was proletarian underdog army town against preening stockbroker-belt wide boys. It didn't feel like that from where I was standing. What it felt like was resurgent, newly-promoted Aldershot, with sackfuls of chips on their shoulders, about to be deeply unpleasant to poor little on-their-uppers Woking. On a day of monsoon conditions in Hampshire we drew 0-0 against them on a pitch you could have grown rice on. More people watched it than any previous post-war qualifying round game (6,870). In retrospect, I've no idea why.

In the replay, the unthinkable happened. They took the lead, inevitably through Abbott, and the abyss yawned. I felt myself thinking that was finally that. The bragging rights had gone. We were no longer the daddies. Not only would we not be in the first round for the first time since 1988-89, we'd have gone out to that lot from down the road. Thankfully, George thought otherwise. Aldershot took the field for the second half in an unconventional 8-1-1 formation, we got the upper hand, nicked an equaliser and won it in extra time. Apocalypse postponed. We went out in the first round proper, 1-0 at home to Scunthorpe, with profound gratitude.

It isn't just Aldershot. Geoff Chapple continues to haunt us. Having left Woking after the club failed to offer him a contract – which he suddenly felt he needed after 12 years without one – he's turned up in charge of Kingstonian. Whether his new club will give him the room to improve on Woking's Conference achievements remains to be seen. An FA Trophy win (his fourth in six years), a decent cup run and eighth place overall (one above us) have caused as much unease at Kingfield as they have joy in Kingston. More, probably: Ks have never been ones for noisy celebration.

Everywhere we seem to turn nowadays, there are unwelcome visitors. Sutton United, former uncontested lords of Surrey non-League, are back. It's the only name on the fixture list that makes me want to hide under the table in whimpering terror, despite the fact that we haven't played them competitively for six years.

And yet somehow the future doesn't look as unremittingly dire as it did when I sat in the car after Barrow. We've got a solid squad, and if they aren't ever going to produce the cavalier stuff in which Chapple's sides specialised, they at least perform as a unit, know how to grind out the one-nils and might just surprise a few folk next year. Maybe even me. Perhaps the readjustment of expectation is the greatest achievement of the McGovern period. We no longer feel that next year will be ours, definitely, and somehow the atmosphere about the club is the more wholesome for it.

The new manager Brian McDermott, himself the victim of a sad sequence of events which saw Slough Town ejected from the Conference, has the broad support of most fans – itself a notable change from the divisions which have been the norm. There's talk of rebuilding a proper, coherent youth policy, in which the manager would have a big say. We're often seen as a lucky club. McDermott's availability at a time when we were floundering might prove to be the biggest stroke yet.

For the club's overall future, it is worth noting that the interest payments on that new stand only become due if we achieve League status (some cheerful souls still say "when", bless 'em). It might be worth hanging around in the Conference after all. Hell, without all the overheated expectations of the past decade we might even learn to enjoy being mid-table. Never mind "doing a Wycombe", we could be the new Northwich Victoria, us. And thoughts turn to another club who had a much worse seventh season in their first stint in the Conference, ending in relegation: Cheltenham Town. Wonder what happened to them?

noises off
uli hesse-lichtenberger

German football spent most of the season getting bitchy and hot under the collar – about almost everything except football

Ah, so close, so very close!

It would have taken only a few honest men to save the 1998-99 Bundesliga season. For had the hoary honourables who claim to run the DFB (the German FA) followed the letter of the law we would have been presented with one of the all-time great trivia questions: Name the Bundesliga game in which five goals were scored yet both teams lost 2-0. Instead, those petty-minded and stubborn bureaucrats applied common sense for the first time in living memory and ruined everything.

On September 26th, VfL Bochum travelled to Kaiserslautern. Actually, that's the first hitch right there, as Bochum didn't have to travel. They had beaten Kaiserslautern four days earlier in the Cup and decided to stay in the city of the defending champions to prepare for the league match, hoping for a repeat of their surprise victory.

The game in question saw the home side take the lead after only five minutes. Then, after 39 minutes, Kaiserslautern's Danish man-marker

Michael Schjönberg found a hole in the Bochum defence and himself in a good scoring position. Bochum's keeper Thomas Ernst left his goal in a desperate attempt to block the shot. He collided with Schjönberg and both players went down, Ernst because he had been hit in the head, Schjönberg because the impact had smashed his leg to smithereens.

When Kaiserslautern's coach Otto Rehhagel realised the graveness of Schjönberg's injury, he signalled for a substitute. The man of his choice was Pascal Ojigwe, a Nigerian. Ojigwe came on as Schjönberg was carried off and play resumed. That's when it dawned on Kaiserslautern's officials that they suddenly had four non-EU foreigners on the field – the Egyptians Hany Ramzy and Ibrahim Samir, the Brazilian Ratinho and Ojigwe. Under DFB regulations, the game would automatically be recorded as a 2-0 win to Bochum as soon as the away team filed a protest.

Rehhagel attempted to save what was already beyond hope by ordering Ramzy to fake an injury. Four minutes after the first, fateful substitution, Ramzy hobbled off in a brave display of the actor's craft and was replaced by the undoubtedly German Harry Koch. However, it was too late. During the break, Bochum's business manager Klaus Hilpert informed his team of what had happened and that the match was won. In the second half, Kaiserslautern made it 2-0 but then succumbed to a Bochum side freed of all restrictions. The visitors scored three times in the last 30 minutes to win the game fair and square. Elated, the club decided not to file a protest in order to spare Kaiserslautern further humiliation.

Up to this point, the affair was merely an embarrassment to Rehhagel and a possible footnote for statistical yearbooks. It certainly wasn't an oddity. Eight other German clubs had already fallen victim to this particular technicality – many fans will remember the game between Stuttgart and Leeds in 1992 which saw Christoph Daum giving away the chance of entry into the Champions League by bringing on a fourth foreigner seven minutes from time.

But the story had only just begun. Because there was still the matter of Bochum's goalkeeper. During half-time, Ernst complained of dizziness on account of the collision and was given a cardiac stimulant by the physio. His condition improved, and he was able to finish the game. Fate had it that Ernst was chosen for random drug testing after the match. Five weeks later the DFB announced they had found a mild dose of a forbidden substance in Ernst's urine sample. Under DFB regulations, the game was automatically lost by a score of 2-0 should Kaiserslautern file a protest. Which they did. Bochum retaliated by retrospectively protesting against Kaiserslautern's use of four non-EU foreigners, and the mess was complete.

The DFB scheduled a hearing for mid-November to decide the matter. It took the judges seven hours of cross-examination and discussion to come up with a solution. The original result was allowed to stand, as it had been established beyond doubt that all blame for Ernst's misfortune lay with the physio and that this wasn't a case of intentional doping. The club was fined DM80,000 (£30,000), for stupidity I presume, and that was that. Everybody in German football lauded the verdict as sensible and fair.

Except me, of course. First, because my sense of the absurd had been insulted. Second, because it was news to me that it's no longer enough to prove doping, now we also have to prove it was done intentionally (a lot of weight-lifters and sprinters will be happy to hear this). Third, because I considered it irresponsible that a player who was showing symptoms of a possibly serious problem was rashly stuffed with medicine and sent out to play on in a game which had already been rendered meaningless. Call me a wimp, but we've had deaths on football pitches before.

The only substantial consequence was that the reportedly troubled Reebok company used it as an excuse to cancel its kit deal with Bochum (saving itself more than DM750,000). And yet this aborted courtroom drama summed up the whole season. Nothing was as gripping as promised and everything of interest happened off the pitch.

For all practical purposes, all on-the-field matters were settled as early as February 20th, when Bayern Munich, notoriously slow re-starters, won their first match after the winter break, 3-0 at Duisburg, to go ten points clear at the top. I watched the game from the press box, and the longer it lasted the more palpable became a gloomy pall that hung over even hardened journalists as it dawned on them that these two teams were inhabitating parallel but different universes. At times I felt like watching my son's team when they are up against boys two years older. It wasn't that Duisburg were having a particularly bad day or Bayern a good one. It was just another nine-to-five day at the office in a league which consisted of 17 football clubs and Bayern Munich.

Downstairs, Mönchengladbach, Frankfurt, Nuremberg and Rostock all failed to win, which made it look almost certain the three relegation victims would be found among this foursome, at least until Bochum began to disintegrate in April. In the event, the last day of the season saw five clubs engaged in a gripping struggle to avoid the final relegation place, which ended with Jan Åge Fjortoft's 87th- minute goal for Eintracht in a 5-1 defeat of Kaiserslautern keeping them up at the expense of Nuremburg on goals scored.

But for most of the season the suspense seemed limited to watching 13 clubs compete for up to nine places promising entry into Europe. Like, wow. In practice, nobody cared. Spot checks carried out by myself on the Dortmund terraces revealed that just about everybody had completely lost track of who could qualify for what, not to mention how and why. And it wasn't only the fans who felt that way. When a smart-aleck reporter asked 1860 Munich's coach Werner Lorant whether he was aware his team could sneak into the UEFA Cup by way of the fair play trophy, Lorant gawped into the void, then sneered: "Fair play? I don't even know what that is, 'fair play'!"

Gradually, those observers relatively free of vested interests (ie those not working for the tabloids or private television) began using terms such as "boring" and "a drag" about league football. The season was only ten weeks young when a sports weekly said it all seemed "strangely lifeless", which was a cautious way of stating that everybody – fans, players, journalists – appeared to be going through the motions.

On one day in March, seven of the nine half-time scores were 0-0.

Nothing an Italian would lose sleep over, but cause for concern in the Bundesliga, which usually tops the big European leagues in goals scored per game. Then there were the gates for 1860 Munich, a tradition-laden club with a huge local following, which were actually down from last year during the first half of the season, when it appeared the club would make it into Europe.

There was the fact that spring came to the continent's biggest television market without UEFA having been able to find a station willing to broadcast the oh-so-attractive revamped Champions League at the new going rates. Finally, there were Bremen's business manager Willi Lemke and Kaiserslautern's director Jürgen Friedrich, who perfectly caught the prevailing mood when making predictions concerning the future of the league. Lemke was talking about the possible end of selling TV rights collectively, Friedrich about losing young prospects to richer clubs. Both, however, used precisely the same term: "It's no longer any fun."

All this might have been attributed to a case of World Cup hangover, but nothing comparable had happened after Italia 90 and USA 94. On the contrary: the two seasons following these tournaments had been spectatcular, dramatic affairs, both decided on the final day and neither won by Bayern.

And yet the World Cup did play a role. It wasn't a hangover, but rather a sobering up. The inept performances of the national team (coupled with its disgraceful behaviour) in France opened many an eye to what lay beyond the dayglo football wonderland of Nike ads and pay-per-view campaigns – reality. And reality was best summed up by ex-international Hans-Peter Briegel after Germany lost 3-0 to the US and drew 3-3 with ten Colombians: "German football," he said, "is no more than mediocre."

Mediocre. If there is a single word business people and PR-men dread more than, say, "tax investigation", then it's "mediocre". You can sell the best and the worst, the prettiest and the ugliest. But the mundane, the average – that's a surefire loser, especially to an audience brought up on hype and coming with high expectations. For the first time this decade merchandise sales stagnated, then began to sink. So did the TV ratings. The market was saturated, economists explained. "The market" means people. "Saturated" means sick.

Thank God for boardrooms. While what some writers stubbornly insisted on calling "the football" dragged itself along, the officials filled the breach, obviously feeling that if the players failed to entertain it was their duty to offer relief – comic or tragic, depending on your viewpoint.

The show hit the road in September when Berti Vogts stepped down and the DFB began what one paper labelled "a grotesque win-a-manager tombola". Egidius Braun, president of the DFB, offered Vogts's former post to people too numerous to mention here, Roy Hodgson and Paul Breitner among them. Finally he settled on the semi-retired Erich Ribbeck and on Uli Stielike, who in the span of one year had been fired by one club in the German Third Division and another in the Spanish Second.

The press conference at which the duo was presented had Pythonesque qualities. One reporter asked Ribbeck if he was still in touch with the modern game, having spent the past two years on a Spanish island playing golf. "I read the papers and some football magazines," Ribbeck replied. "I know what's going on."

In October the DFB held its annual meeting and changed its statutes to allow clubs to become limited companies. That was not an easy thing to do for an organisation steeped so deeply in the amateur spirit that it fought professionalism until the Sixties. But the pressure from clubs eager to get to the fleshpots had become so intense that the DFB felt it would risk a hostile split by insisting on obsolete values.

Once this path was cleared, however, the usual suspects – Bayern and Dortmund – suddenly declared they were in no hurry to change their status. Bayern said they didn't need the money yet; Dortmund said they would wait for the right moment, meaning success on the pitch. Thus the first German club to become a company was Berlin. Not Hertha, mind you, but unhip and badly supported Tennis Borussia. Meanwhile, Sepp Blatter got down to business and suggested novelties only the most dedicated could keep track of: a World Cup every two years, domestic seasons beginning in February, leagues reduced to 16 teams, a World Club Championship held in some exotic place and assorted other brainwaves.

The German public became convinced Blatter had gone stark raving mad, and relatively independent-minded officials like Dortmund's president Dr Gerd Niebaum got fed up: "FIFA must stop issuing regulations without consulting anybody first," he said, adding a threat: "None of us would have a problem with recognising UEFA as our main governing body instead of FIFA."

The DFB, however, were caught between a rock and a hard place. Braun, some say, is a man too honest for his job, a man who had lobbied for Lennart Johansson to become FIFA's president instead of Blatter. It seems highly likely Braun was as furious as anyone else at Blatter – only he couldn't say so. Why? Beckenbauer will tell you. "We must stop laying into FIFA," he pleaded. "Otherwise our chances of getting the World Cup in 2006 are very slim." Ah, the wonderfully wicked world of diplomacy. More thrilling than many football games, certainly more thrilling than the football games of this season. Small wonder, then, that people became more interested in the men in suits than those in short trousers.

In January, television took over the agenda, as the league and the DFB tried to arrange new rights deals. The problem was that the EU still hadn't decided whether or not the DFB's central marketing was an infringement on the individual clubs' freedom of enterprise. To crown this bizarre stalemate, UEFA couldn't come to terms with RTL Television about what the blown-up Champions League was worth. Currently, RTL pays DM100 million a year – and loses DM50 million. Now UEFA wanted DM250 million, which raised laughter at RTL's headquarters. So UEFA contacted other German channels, all of which declined.

Then, on May 3rd, UEFA announced they had at long last found a taker. The name of that taker came as a shock to even the best-informed pinstripes. It was neither of the two German global media players,

Bertelsmann (owners of RTL) and the Kirch group (owners of SAT1 and holder of the European rights to the 2002 World Cup). The Champions League, UEFA beamed, would go to the largely unknown channel TM3 – a station whose only claim to fame was that it attracted a minority following of trash connoisseurs who found perverse pleasure in watching crappy films in between features on cooking, hairdressing and Japanese flower-arranging.

In fact, when the story broke, most people considered it a practical joke, as TM3 didn't even have an editorial office for sport. Then, however, a name began making the rounds, and suddenly it all fell into place. It was the name of Rupert Murdoch, who six months earlier had bought 66 per cent of TM3. **TV-Shark Invades Germany** headlined the tabloid *Bild*, and once again the actual football had been demoted to a side topic. At least the furore generated the quote of the year, when Leo Kirch, the man who gave Germany the Bundesliga show that has more commercials than football, said: "UEFA have unmasked themselves. They only care about money."

In early May, on the occasion of a game between Bayer Leverkusen and Bremen, Leverkusen's business manager Rainer Calmund faced the press to answer questions about the match. Instead he was asked about shares and replica shirts, Braun and Blatter, pay-per-view and public relations.

"This is about football!" he exploded. "Football has to be the centre of attention, otherwise we might as well shut up shop."

Calmund, one has to understand, is known here as "the man with the suitcase" – meaning a suitcase full of money to buy talented youngsters. He is the man who transformed Leverkusen's cosy Ulrich Haberland Stadium into the "BayArena", a posh assemblage of glass-panelled VIP boxes and the league's first all-seater ground.

"If somebody like Karel van Miert [the EU's competition commissioner] is suddenly better known than 100 of our footballers, then we're on the wrong track," Calmund added. The journos gravely nodded their heads.

This was three days after Nuremberg had filed a protest with the

DFB over their game against Dortmund, claiming the home fans had created such a din that "the players had been unable to concentrate on the game". Concentrate on the game? Now there's a revolutionary thought.

ambitions
hampered

mark tallentire

Everton fans hoped for an upturn in their fortunes. Peter Johnson hoped for a £60 million pay-off. Both were to be disappointed

When Walter Smith paid for and sent out three cases of Dommelsch for the 200 or so Everton fans lounging on the garden furniture behind the goal at the Dutch amateur club UNA in August 1998, he would have been hoping that the task of serving up the on-pitch cheer could be achieved as easily. Smith, after all, had just become the first leading Scottish manager to take up a position south of the border since Graeme Souness, his former No 1 at Rangers, arrived at Anfield seven years earlier, and the feelgood factor among those in Veldhoven that night was almost tangible.

The Scot, who was on the verge of taking the Sheffield Wednesday manager's job rather than a back seat to Dick Advocaat at Ibrox, had accepted the Everton owner-chairman Peter Johnson's £750,000-a-year, three-season deal – twice the Hillsborough offer – at the 11th hour after Leicester's Martin O'Neill had joined the ranks of those to reject overtures from the hamper magnate. Johnson pledged the £20 million transfer budget Smith had demanded to secure a Premiership top-ten place and within days the new manager had spent a total of £9.1 million on three ball-players: Marco Materazzi, John Collins and Olivier Dacourt.

"Everton have been there and want to get back," Smith commented when he became the club's fourth manager in five seasons. Eight months later his words could easily have been interpreted as a reflection on life in the second tier, which Everton left in 1954 and with which they were again flirting dangerously.

This had become the way of things since 1994, when Johnson got his hands on the club for £10 million. The son of a Toxteth butcher, Johnson made his money in the food-packaging industry and was then reputed to be worth £120 million, based on the stock value of his company, Park Foods. As chairman of Tranmere Rovers he had revitalised the club, upgraded Prenton Park and bankrolled an ageing team through the leagues into the First Division by 1992.

However, seeing bigger pickings across the Mersey, he engaged in an unsavoury power struggle with the then Everton director Bill Kenwright to take control of the club after the death of the majority shareholder, Sir John Moores. Although it had been Moores's declared wish that his shares should go to a person with Everton's best interests at heart, it was Johnson (who had previously advertised in the press for Liverpool shares) who won the day after bidding Kenwright up from £3 million to £10 million and promising to invest further cash.

The Wirral grocer announced he would be continuing with his day-to-day business while taking control of a club he would regard as a "hobby", but with whom he intended to win the European Cup. John Moores, the Liverpool-supporting son of Sir John, was later honest enough to admit: "I have never forgiven myself for selling my shares to Peter Johnson, but I thought I was doing what my father would have wanted." As for Smith, who was beguiled by similar bullish platitudes from Johnson five years later, he would be looking for a new team captain in November when the sale of Duncan Ferguson to Newcastle was sanctioned by the chairman while the manager was sitting on the bench supervising the first home win of the season, against the Geordies. Ferguson's sale triggered Johnson's resignation as chairman and the club was again put up for sale.

From then on, Smith was forced to rummage around in the bargain basement, relying on the youth team, loan signings and players who would be out of contract in the summer and available at knock-down fees. By the season's end, Johnson's position had become increasingly precarious as the value of his shareholdings plummeted and the Labour MP for Walton, Peter Kilfoyle, fired off letters to all and sundry questioning the integrity of Johnson's business practices. Kilfoyle wrote to the FA, the Premier League and the Nationwide League to ask what action would be being taken against Johnson, who had been told to drop his interest in either Everton or Tranmere before December 31st 1998.

On that Veldhoven evening, however, the positive mood represented a huge upturn from the vagaries of the previous season, when Johnson had forced the then incumbent Howard Kendall to operate on a budget befitting a club in the First Division, a destination which they only avoided on goal difference. Smith, who had been involved with nine championship winning sides in successive seasons at Ibrox, had the credentials to pull the club out of a tail-spin rooted in Colin Harvey's elevation to the manager's office when Howard Kendall left for Athletic Bilbao in May 1987.

However, it took only a matter of weeks for Smith to become aware of the true nature of his relationship with Johnson. The manager's next foray into the market, the £3 million signing of the club's former player David Unsworth, had all the hallmarks of the Johnson years. It took three weeks to conclude due to the chairman being incommunicado and the defender not surprisingly felt that Everton were not following through their initial interest. Unsworth left West Ham for Aston Villa before Johnson reaffirmed an interest, and the player returned to Everton after one reserve game for Villa.

The England Under-21 goalkeeper Steve Simonsen was next to arrive, from Johnson's "other" club Tranmere, in a convoluted deal initially said to be worth £3.3 million. However, Rovers manager John Aldridge, who was forced to hunt around for a loan goalkeeper before the deal could go through, subsequently blew the whistle and declared it to be worth only £500,000, which would rise to £3.3 million in the event of Simonsen having a successful Everton and England career. He did not play a first-team game last season.

If Smith had not realised problems were in the offing he soon saw the writing on the wall in late September when a £4.25 million deal was all but concluded with Newcastle for Steve Watson, only for the manager to find the coffers all but empty. Watson joined Villa instead. What transpired to be Smith's final big signing – and his worst – was the arrival of Ibrahima Bakayoko for £4.5 million from Montpellier to partner Ferguson.

He made his debut in the home game against Liverpool, another 0-0, and managed to miss an open goal from eight yards. Cameos in the away games at Bristol City in the FA Cup and Blackburn in the league could not disguise the fact that he and English football were ill-suited. Regardless of Bakayoko's efforts on the pitch, it proved to be a deal too far for the club's bankers and Ferguson's £8 million sale was sanctioned on November 23rd while Everton, without the injured captain, were beating Newcastle 1-0.

"If it had been up to me, I would have kept Duncan," said Smith at the time. After a meeting with Johnson in London five days later – on the eve of the away match at Charlton, which prompted a huge demonstration against the chairman by the travelling fans – Smith returned to Scotland for a family funeral and vowed not to return unless Johnson made a public proclamation that it was he and not the manager who had brokered the deal. Johnson, under duress, finally did so and an hour later released a statement saying he was stepping down, citing health reasons. "The role has become increasingly arduous since he moved to Jersey," it read. At the same time, he let it be known he was prepared to sell his stake. Sums of up to £60 million were bandied about.

"I'm absolutely delighted for Everton fans; but they mustn't get carried away because he's still got 68 per cent of the shareholding and so, ultimately, still has the final say," said Andy Gray, another to have rejected Johnson's overtures the previous summer, when he was searching for a successor to Joe Royle.

It was a timely warning, but for the time being the crisis seemed worse on the pitch than off. After 11 home league games which yielded three Everton goals, one a penalty, Smith could reflect that he had presided over the worst home sequence in Everton's 121-year history. One local bookmaker stopped taking bets on 0-0 draws having paid out on six occasions already. After the seventh, with Leicester in January, Tony Cottee, who scored 72 league goals for Everton from 1988-94 and whose sale to West Ham was sanctioned with typical foresight two weeks before Ferguson's arrival, said: "Some crowds would turn against a team who are struggling at home. Everton's are reasonably patient; they know it's not a quick fix."

It is not a slow one, either. Everton have become a standing joke in the transfer market, the disciplinary record is at an all-time low, the club's marketing operation is more Sixties than Nineties – the ticket office does not even take credit card bookings over the phone. Despite having to endure Liverpool's unparalleled 15 years of success through the Seventies and Eighties, Everton supporters are used to, and expect, better. But even though attendances are at a post-war high, things have never been worse.

The sale of Ferguson, albeit at a commanding price for an under-achieving crock, rankled, as the money was used to reduce the overdraft rather than strengthen the team. By now, Johnson's price had come down to £43 million – still a record for a Premiership club. Kenwright was still the only interested suitor but with the overdraft rising and team strengthening impossible he lost the backing of HSBC when it realised that the club's debts would be approaching £20 million by the summer. Worse still, there was little prospect of that amount being reduced, short of asset-stripping a team with a wage bill of £13.85 million.

Smith was left penniless and fighting for the club's Premiership life. But for the emergence of the youth team striker Francis Jeffers, who scored Everton's first goal of the season at the Gwladys Street end on February 11th, and the good fortune that Kevin Campbell fell out with Trabzonspor and was available on loan, relegation was well and truly on the cards.

Nine goals from Campbell and five from his young foil saved the day. Everton peeled off three straight wins in April after slipping into the bottom three for six days following an inept 2-1 reverse at home to Sheffield Wednesday. Fellow strugglers Charlton, meanwhile, were winning at West Ham courtesy of Graham Stuart, the last-day saviour of Mike Walker's Everton in a May 1994 victory over Wimbledon.

Which was where Johnson came in. The only comfort to be taken from the club's situation was that his dreams of departing with a cheque for £60 million in his back pocket were rapidly subsiding. As the City cooled on football as an investment vehicle, it was becoming increasingly apparent that Johnson would be lucky to get back what he put into the club, the initial £10 million plus a secondary injection of around £9 million in 1995.

When Everton travelled to Old Trafford in April still in desperate need of points for survival, Manchester United's manager Alex Ferguson said the game would have a big bearing on his club's Treble ambitions. Not because of its degree of difficulty, obviously, but because it came just days after United's successful trip to the San Siro for the European Cup semi-final, second leg. Could their players motivate themselves to pick up three points from a game of such relative mundanity? United, despite resting several first-teamers, duly completed a run-of-the-mill 3-1 victory.

Back in 1985 it had been Ron Atkinson's ten-man United side who were lucky to deprive a weary Everton of a significant treble thanks to Norman Whiteside's extra-time winner three days after the Blues had won the Cup-Winners Cup and before that the league with a then-record 90 points.

It was to Smith's credit that despite an early predilection for being too cagey at home and packing the midfield with central defenders, he led the club to the FA Cup quarter-finals and then to Premiership safety with the comparative luxury of a week to spare. Such is the decline of one of the so-called Big Five that that record has to be considered a success.

we are the world
matthew hall

The power of television means domestic leagues in weaker countries are exposed to competition from the Premiership. Not surprisingly, they're losing

The bloke who called up the radio station's football phone-in show was raving. He was almost scary, seemingly beamed in direct from an earlier appearance on some long ago cancelled Seventies TV sitcom. One so bad that even cable stations desperate to fill all available air time with "ironic" nostalgia would have steered clear of it. On he ranted: "They've come over here, they've taken all our jobs, it's no longer an English game..."

Claiming to support neither Manchester United, Arsenal nor Chelsea, but rather Sheffield Wednesday, Mr Cranky of Woking added that the sudden rush of foreign players into the Premiership had resulted in the "English game no longer being the domain of the Englishman". Sure, football had come home, he reasoned, but what about the penny-pinching riff-raff it had brought along with it?

The show's host paid short courtesy to the caller before moving swiftly along to ask whether Gérard Houllier was, in fact, Christian Gross in disguise. A pity, really, because despite the caller's Union

Jack boxer shorts diverting his train of thought, he had hit a nail right on the head. It may come as a surprise but, sure enough, the Premiership is no longer solely an English domain. The shock for Mr Cranky, though, is that the evidence is not to be found on Saturday afternoon teamsheets.

Football history will record Wednesday May 26th 1999 as the day Manchester United finally recaptured their Holy Grail – the European Cup, or whatever it's called this year. Probably less than 50,000 people in the stadium were there exclusively to support the English team but around the world, in Salford, Hackney, Bondi, Brooklyn, Dublin and Delhi, people perched in front of TV sets and willed on their red, white and black heroes. These fans weren't singing Bavarian beer tunes. It was the red of Manchester they supported. And there was a very good reason for it. Television.

It was no different in a bar in Boston, New England, recommended by a friend who days earlier had spotted the words chalked on an outside blackboard: "3pm Wednesday – English Soccer Manchester v Munich." The bar was all nooks and crannies, which seemed to exaggerate the crush. Nevertheless, a 100-strong crowd on a workday afternoon was at least ten times more than the usual number of customers here.

"Why the crowd?" I baited the manager behind the bar. "English soccer!" he beamed happily, pointing to the TV in the corner and pulling another pitcher of the local brew. "Would you have the same sized crowd if fate and the draw had tossed up a final between Bayern and Dinamo Kiev?" I probed. The manger looked confused. "Is that English soccer?" he asked.

The answer, of course, is no. Not that the question needed asking. Sure, Dinamo, Bayern and Juventus would have provided just as entertaining a spectacle and all those sides would have lived out their own dramatic soap opera equal to United's crusade. But it was the presence of "Manchester" in Barcelona that had people sitting, standing and ultimately leaping up and down in front of TVs all over the world.

This tale has nothing to do with the tired old jokes about United fans all living outside Manchester. No, this concerns bottom lines. Dollars, euros, the odd pound, the blinkered view of English football observers and the wide-eyed vision of a few suited bean counters. And a few TV sets. Mr Cranky of Woking was right when he suggested that English football is no longer the exclusive domain of the English (and Welsh, Scots and Irish) but it has more to do with a remote control than loss of national identity.

It's no secret that television rights now comprise a significant portion of a football club's income. So significant that Mr Cranky and his ilk must be surprised where clubs like Chelsea get the cash to sign and pay the wages of A-class foreign talent. It's not just domestic TV rights that spin money. Television sets in Liberia flicker and buzz as Monrovia's Ultras follow the fortunes of George Weah at Milan. Similar behaviour occurs in Sydney when Harry Kewell pulls on his Leeds shirt.

In January this year, Croatia Zagreb signed Japan's Kazu Miura as a direct replacement for Mark Viduka, who had finally moved to Celtic. Miura, of course, is a Japanese legend. Earlier in his career he'd taken off for Santos in Brazil and was the first Japanese player in Serie A, with Genoa. Now the wrong side of 30, he had probably thought his chances of playing in the Champions League were a little remote. Until he got a phone call from Zagreb, that is.

Goran Bradic, Croatia Zagreb's press officer, winked mischievously as he explained the surprise addition of Miura to the Croatian flagship club. "It's an inspired signing," he explained, pausing for effect before adding, "... by the marketing department." There was nothing lost in translation. Especially as he grinned as he finished his sentence. TV rights to Japan, you see.

Sure enough, at the weekly Friday morning pre-match press conference, crowded in among the local media were three journalists from Japan sent to track every pass, header, shot and word uttered by Mr Miura. They were most welcome, said Goran Bradic. In fact, with the money that Japanese TV were forking out they were virtual VIPs. The rumours that Alex Ferguson may have found Hidetoshi Nakata thrust into his Old Trafford squad by potential new owners last season may not have been as ludicrous as first thought.

When it comes to worldwide TV audiences, the Premier League's aggressive sales pitch places it on top of the international league. The league markets its own weekly highlights package which is beamed across the US, Asia, Australia and whoever else is buying. In Australia, a one-hour Monday night prime time show replays, in *Match of the Day* style, the highlights from the previous weekend.

The "beauty" of pay TV also means that it's possible to see more live televised Premier League action in Australia than it is in England. Support Manchester United and live in Sheffield? Can't get a ticket to Old Trafford? Move to Perth. The time difference means that at 10pm on a Saturday night you can be on the couch with a cheap six-pack of Fosters watching a Premiership game beamed live from Anfield, Stamford Bridge or Old Trafford, with a delayed telecast of another game set to follow straight after. Then there's always tomorrow's direct feed of *Ford Super Sunday* (and don't think that worldwide Ford awareness wasn't figured in the sponsorship package, neither) if you need a further fix.

Television dollars have such a grip on football that Major League Soccer in the US has come up with a novel way of raising profits for its league. The equation is simple. America contains large pockets of football-mad Latin American communities. Why not host an international fixture between two Central or South American countries and sell the TV rights back to the home nations? In late May this year, New York/New Jersey Metrostars hosted New England Revolution as the first half of a double header. The "tie" also featured a friendly between Colombia and El Salvador. Over 40,000 people packed into Giants Stadium for the games, double usual MLS attendance figures. The MLS laughed its way to the bank with the profits made from selling TV rights to stations in San Salvador and Bogotá.

Advances in communications make the world a truly smaller place, but they also open up tricky issues that could suggest a new world order of commercial and cultural imperialism. The British empire is alive and well but it resembles nothing like what was taught in school. Pick up a Sydney newspaper on a Monday morning and the English

Premiership dominates the reporting of "soccer". Already struggling to compete against Australian Rules and Murdoch-monied rugby league, domestic football is relegated way back within the sports pages to fight it out with golf and horse racing.

Within its allotted space, the local national league is then pitted against European and English leagues. Why bother reading about the next Harry Kewell or Mark Bosnich when the current exploits of today's superstars are so readily accessible? That's if Cole and Yorke or Owen and Fowler aren't grabbing headlines. When a monthly glossy called *Soccer Australia* features Kevin Keegan as its cover star, the local league must surely know it's in a trench war for attention.

It's not just within the media that the Empire strikes back. Leeds and West Ham both have well-established connections with junior clubs in New South Wales and Western Australia. While the Hammers have generally been well received and have made an effort to score good PR with local communities, the recruitment activities of Leeds have drawn the ire of Australian authorities. O'Leary's "kids" may receive accolades from all and sundry in the UK for their plucky spirit, and the club may be congratulated in some quarters for their foresight and faith in promoting young talent, but outside Britain you'll hear allegations of player poaching, exploitation of other countries' youth systems and outright disregard for the greater good of the game.

It's a dizzy old circle. Local leagues surrender media space and their best players to international giants. Following rapidly out the door are the spectators who interpret their indigenous product as inferior to the glitz and glamour they see on TV each week. Why watch South Melbourne when Liverpool will be on in ten minutes? Desperate people do desperate things and cash-starved football clubs are no different. Struggling clubs court relationships with big European brothers.

In Australia, this has manifested itself with clubs like the Melbourne Knights and West Adelaide, traditionally "ethnic" clubs based in the Croatian and Greek communities respectively, offering themselves as feeders to Manchester United and Celtic. These clubs are so desperate for cash injections they even talk of prostituting their own traditional strips in favour of wearing United or Celtic colours. It's not just Australia where this is occurring but also South Africa and even Belgium. It's franchise football as diverse and risk-free as a McDonalds or Pizza Hut outlet.

If it's not a direct relationship with a British club then it's corporate investment. In its first year of operation, Sydney club Northern Spirit courted major investment from a certain M Goldberg of south London which might have led to him becoming the major shareholder. Thankfully for the Australian club, as Goldberg's personal fortune plummeted, his interest in Northern Spirit became legally problematic, allowing the club's owners to dilute their relationship with King-Midas-in-reverse and offer the club's coaching staff and senior players (including Robbie Slater and Ian Crook) the chance to buy into their own club.

In July, Manchester United took a by-pass from the usual route for pre-season tours. Instead of a trip to Norway or Ireland, the Treble winners embarked on a 24-hour flight to Australia. The deal was inked dry long before United had an established connection with the antipodes through Mark Bosnich. Obviously, the £2 million on offer from an Australian promoter for a couple of games in Melbourne and Sydney proved a good enough incentive for United plc to make United FC available for what was essentially a meet-and-greet with United's far-flung fan base.

The two exhibition games drew crowds of around 70,000 which, except for the four-yearly World Cup qualifying play-offs, are attendances unheard of at Australian soccer matches. How great is United's reach? Rene Rivkin, the private promoter responsible for bringing them to Australia, considered that when European clubs declined to release their Australian stars to play for the Socceroos against United, his gate takings would not be even slightly affected.

"The 150,000 people who have bought tickets so far are going to see Manchester United not the Australian Socceroos," he told ABC radio in the lead-up to the games. "I don't regard Harry Kewell and Mark Viduka as crowd-pullers."

This came as news to the commercial managers of those particular players and their sponsors but underlines the bigger picture. United banked a whopping big cheque just for turning up and Rivkin quietly thanked the Premier League for their foresight in aggressively pursuing an international audience.

Undoubtedly, United's antipodean games passed by Mr Angry of Woking. He was right, though, when he phoned up the radio talk show. English football is no longer England's game. It's far more important than that. Jumpers are no longer adequate for goalposts. Dollar signs work far better.

glory finder
rob chapman

For fairweather fans, there was never a better season to be grateful they had decided to follow Manchester United

Let me nauseate you, as Robbie Williams once sang. I am a Manchester United supporter. From the south.

I could try to appease you by stating that I live within a crowd's roar of Old Trafford, but let's take the scenic route shall we? When I was a kid I used to support Spurs. And in between I had the best part of two decades off.

Are there others out there like me? I certainly never meet them. I meet plenty of post-Hornby, post-Italia 90 converts. And I still meet plenty who never once strayed from the fold. The ones who know the names of obscure Crewe full backs who scored injury-time winners in the days when substitute was singular not plural.

Not me. I popped out for 20 Kensitas some time in the early Seventies and didn't get back until Wimbledon won the Cup. Between 1964 and 1972 I spent 90 per cent of my childhood weekends watching live football of some description. And for nigh on 20 years after that I was one of the missing millions.

True, that demographic shift was well under way before I joined the exodus. But when my number was called, boy did my indifference kick in with a vengeance. By the mid-Eighties I would not have crossed the road to watch a match. I can verify this, as I lived in a house that backed on to St James Park, Northampton, and when I was woken on Sunday mornings by referees' whistles and people shouting "pass it fatty" it was as much as I could do to haul myself to the window to open the curtains. My route back to the fold is filled with the same corny reasons as lots of other people's, but the half a lifetime in the middle has left me with some explaining to do. To myself.

As a kid I invested a lot of misplaced trust in integrity and loyalty. When a childhood friend stopped supporting Man Utd and switched his allegiance to Arsenal, because that's who all his mates supported, it seemed to me the height of betrayal – even though none of us came from these places. So when Spurs replaced Bill Nicholson a couple of years later with an ex-Arsenal man it was like finding out that Father Christmas was just your parents in drag. A couple of years after that Spurs lost their place in the First Division and I drifted off. When allegiance isn't cemented by birthright or religion that's what you do.

I never abandoned football completely, "following" Ipswich in a fairweather sort of way during the Bobby Robson years but the moment that great team broke up, I was off too. I still don't know why. Something to do with Captain Beefheart's worst moves being more interesting than Naylor and Pratt's best ones. Then, of course, there was that Leeds fan who put a knife to my throat in the subway on King's Cross station. But one blade-wielding Yorkshire ripper doesn't make you abandon a teenage passion and I suspect that my tactical withdrawal was at an advanced planning stage well before that incident.

As a kid my allegiances went up in geopolitical tiers. My local town team was Sandy Albion of the South Midlands League. On Sunday mornings we watched half of our Sandy heroes turn out for neighbouring village team Potton Casuals, and on Sunday afternoons we watched the Sunday pub team of all Sunday pub teams, Gobion Goblins. Next up was my nearest large town team, Bedford of the Southern

League; a couple of decent Cup runs in the 1960s and a glimpse of a 16-year-old called Steve Perryman playing for Spurs A team against Bedford reserves. Next step up was my nearest league club, Luton. The Malcolm MacDonald years and "Harry Roberts is our friend". If anyone remembers a low-budget George Best called Graham French, I am available for dewy-eyed reminiscences at the drop of a Hatter.

And sitting on top of all that? Glory, Glory Tottenham Hotspur. Like any other eight-year-old I must have turned to my Dad circa 1961 and said: "Fear not father for my destiny lies at the sign of a cockerel crowing." Or words to that effect. And do you know, I was true to my infant word right up until they got relegated.

Mine was no Damascene reconversion. Not for me the beloved route of celebrities such as Michael Nyman, who say things like: "I was practising my avante garde scales one day, heard the delightful noise from Loftus Road and I've been a fan ever since." Nor the laddish affections of TV personalities who were busy studying mediaeval English at Cambridge when Frank Worthington was shagging for England, but are now finally having their adolescence in their thirties.

I distrust people who "discover" football in their thirties. It's a bit like discovering sex, or music, or breathing that late in life. Makes you wonder what they were doing before. Still, I suppose you can say the same about people who have the best part of 20 years off and then conveniently reappear when the silverware starts pouring in.

I respond to the "glory-hunting" taunts with the only ammunition I've got. First, I could have supported Liverpool at any time in those 15 years of European and domestic domination, but didn't. They were the progressive rock of football. Note perfect, but where was the soul? Efficient? Sure. Flawless? Often. But unpredictability? Eccentricity? Wayward genius? I had to wait for that. Second, and far more pertinently, in this age of geographical mobility and socio-economic fluidity, I ask in all seriousness: where does the uprooted exile go? Well, this one ended up in Manchester in 1991, on the back of the Cup-Winners Cup victory. After two years of poll tax avoiding and spiral tribing, Ravechester felt like home.

As a kid United were the only team I respected. The only team I fervently wanted Spurs to beat. All the joy of winning the FA Cup in 1967 was diluted because the Reds won the league. But while I was out getting the Kensitas some strange things happened. United didn't just lose their invincibility. They went down to the Second Division. A generation of hardened drinkers came and went. Only months before I moved to Manchester I turned on *Match of the Day* one night to be greeted with the sight of United fielding a side of schoolkids. Blimey, they're bonkers aren't they? The seeds were sown. Within six months I would be referring to those schoolkids like I knew them personally.

I wasn't won over by reputation or legacy. I was seduced in my armchair, watching telly highlights of awesome victories. The equation was simple. I hadn't been so thrilled by a side since those Greaves-Gilzean-Mackay-Jennings years of the mid-Sixties. This was the real thing again. No glory by association, no inherent desire to bond with victors. Just Sparky and Sharpy and "that boy running down the wing with the wind in his hair".

My support for United was, if anything, galvanised in their darkest hours. When Eric went kung-fu fighting at Palace, every sanctimonious commentator in the country called for his head. Versed as I was in the ways of betrayal and subterfuge I waited for the banishment that never came. Instead, Paddy Crerand stood outside Old Trafford on the lunchtime news the next day and supported his man. My support was cemented by those acts of faith and loyalty and thrived on United's "Everyone hates us we don't care" mentality. To an old punk like me that's grist to the mill. Bad losers? Good, it means they want to win. If I'd wanted a plucky, oh-well-never-mind kind of loser I'd have devoted my middle youth years to Annabel Croft and the lost legions of British tennis.

Since I came back to the fold I've noticed a few changes. You can't walk up to the match like you used to, and it's not as noisy at it used to be, is it? Yes, I'm afraid many of the cliches are true. Four-one up with ten minutes to go against early season league leaders, Charlton. Dwight Yorke's home debut. The away fans start singing "Shit fans, no noise" and you find yourself thinking that they've got a point (ever so quietly, mind, in case you wake anybody).

Who are these people who rush off after 80 minutes? Somebody stop them and do a survey. At the 3-3 against Barcelona they were drifting away in droves. Three-nil up against Blackburn became 3-2 and a tense last ten minutes. Not for the 4.30 merchants it didn't. They were probably in B&Q by the final whistle, or half way down the M6 as the rest of the country would have it.

And so to this season of immortality. The stench of hyprocrisy hung heavy over the pre-season campaign. So many scores to settle. The championship on loan to an Arsenal team that had the temerity not to be dull, making a mockery of old certainties. Then there was the Brylcreem boy affair. As David Beckham walked off that World Cup pitch with the thousand-yard stare in his eyes I knew it would be the making of him. Think Cantona, I thought. Think that it's always darkest before dawn. And he did. And it was.

The demonising of Beckham had nothing to do with his merits as a footballer and everything to do with "no surrender" patriots with small willies, personified perfectly by a West Ham fan sounding off in a pre-season television profile. "We'd be booing him anyway," he said of Beckham's lively reception at Upton Park. Fair enough. Football is a blood sport at the best of times and it needs a regular supply of fresh bait. "But when he puts on the three lions," he slavered, "he lets down England." Yeah, right. And you boost the export drive do you mate?

So we cheered David Beckham to the echo every time he took a corner, every time he split another defence with another precision pass. He got us out of jail from day one against Leicester to nemesis night in the Nou Camp. Next year perhaps the PFA could make their awards at the end of the season.

The doubts about Jaap Stam seemed to centre initially on the fact that he got turned over in the Charity Shield. Big deal! The shield was so charitable when I was a lad that goalkeepers used to score in it (Pat Jennings and Alex Stepney, naturally). My eyes told me immediately that he was going to be a colossus. And an ungainly and unorthodox one at that, stopping the ball with knee, chin or whatever limb happened to be handy.

And then there was Teddy. Watching a perfunctory Boxing Day 3-0 win over Forest we marvelled as Beckham sent down another perfect ball. Perfect, that is, for a man five yards faster than Sheringham. The game was up and we experts knew it. Fast forward to a similarly perfunctory 3-0 against Sheffield Wednesday and Teddy makes one, then scores one on the stroke of half-time. We troop off to tea and toilets singing his name. In the next urinal a fan says in that non-specific way that men adopt in football urinals: "And just to think we've been slagging him off all season." Little did we know, but we'd just witnessed the start of a renaissance. "Little did we know" will do as a suitable catchphrase for the destiny that was slowly unfolding.

When Ole Solskjaer put Liverpool out of the Cup in injury time we all wore the same amazed expression that he did. I actually said to a friend at the time that only winning the Champions League would beat that. A comment that was promptly buried when Ryan Giggs scored his wonder goal against Arsenal. And to think, we scoffed, thinking we'd just witnessed the finest hour, we thought Ole's Cup goal was the height of the season.

After the semi-final victory at Villa Park there was, you'll remember, a totally uneccessary display of jubilation, resulting in fans getting on to the pitch, many armed with scarves, and David Beckham being lofted shoulder high, an incident which could have resulted in long-term injury. Suitably contrite, the next Saturday at Old Trafford we sang: "We've got the worst behaved supporters in the land."

And then, just as I'm growing accustomed to a certain level of excellence, along comes history and blows me away. Although with the scoreboard reading 0-1 as we entered the 90th minute in the Champions League final, I had begun to think that this destiny thing was being a tad overplayed.

The kind of empowerment that the Treble gave us was the right to drive round Stretford at midnight sounding our horns with impunity.

Everything else palls into inarticulacy. On the sunny morning of victory parade day I drove around funky Manchester, blithely aware that none of us could really put into words what we'd witnessed. Not the fans, not the detractors, pathetically whinging to phone-in shows that we'd never replace Peter Schmeichel (they said the same about Cantona, remember) and certainly not the Key 103 knobhead chosen to be master of ceremonies at the MEN Arena, who conveyed our pre-millennial ecstasy by bawling inane platitudes at grown professionals still in the heady throes of sleep deprivation.

And when tomorrow comes, the history books will have been rewritten, the sickos will have frantically updated their Hate Man U websites, and possibly nothing in football will ever make me that happy again. But in the back of my mind time's squeaky chariot forces me to confront the lie I am living. "Surely you were happiest watching Gobion Goblins. 12-1 down at half time. Jumpers for goalposts, eh?" says a plaintive innocent presence, squatting on my shoulder. I tell him to hush in case anyone hears him, but he persists, so I crush him like an ant with my fist.

room at the top
john earls

Luton fans saw their club edge towards oblivion until the departure of chairman David Kohler. With most of the best players gone too, that only left Lennie Lawrence

It all seemed almost depressingly simple in the end. Two hours before the deadline for Luton Town's suitors to get their act together, the night before the new season started, the headline on the local Teletext read: "Time running out for Luton." The next morning? "New deal for Luton."

That came in August 1999, after a season in which the club's administration proved as inept as the team and its management. At least we didn't get relegated. But the worries of the Kenilworth End diehards for much of 1998-99 were more basic: will there still be a club next season? We had been in receivership since March, and the Football League had finally run out of patience but, as is often the way, a buyer for a troubled club was found at literally the last minute. This time, it was a tad more complicated than most deals, as the new buyer and the old chairman were known to hate each other with a passion.

Luton's chief executive David Kohler had fought a losing battle to gain the respect of fans ever since sacking popular manager Jim Ryan in 1991, after a row far too trivial to repeat here. Kohler finally left in nasty circumstances in March, when an unlit letter bomb was posted through his front door. Less than a week later, our last avenue of getting a new ground near Junction 10 of the M1 was rejected. The High Court upheld the Department of Environment's decision to turn down the site on the basis that traffic arrangements weren't good enough. (Yes, near the M1. Don't ask.)

The battle to get that particular site had been going on for four years, with the support of the town's two MPs and local council. When it was lost, Kohler claimed he wanted a buyer found for the club at the earliest opportunity, so he could finally leave us ungrateful fans to it and never again have to turn up to his offices, where he was employed on a handsome wage as chief executive.

Long-time director Cliff Bassett, whose firm Universal Salvage Auctions were our kit sponsors, immediately tried to do a deal. Kohler said the offer was derisory, Bassett intimated it was his money that had been keeping Luton afloat most of the time Kohler was in charge. The duo stopped speaking and we were officially in receivership. Bassett announced USA wouldn't sponsor the kit in 1999-2000 and the already sagging results got much, much worse.

To be honest, only the mimsiest supporters ever really though we'd get relegated. We'd already built up enough points from our false-dawn promotion campaign that had fallen apart at Christmas, coinciding with the sale of magnificent captain Steve Davis back to his old club Burnley. We finished 12th.

The only real talking point on the pitch was the continued ineptness of manager Lennie Lawrence. Defender Chris Willmott, who was sold to Wimbledon in the close-season, looked England-class every time he played for us. Problem was, Lawrence only picked him for the first time when inconsistent and (admittedly undeservedly) hated first-choice right-back Graham Alexander was sold to Preston on transfer-deadline day.

True, Willmott had had injury problems but why he wasn't given more games with us before March will remain yet another black mark against Lawrence, who was absurdly kind to our defence. The guilty included the depressing sight of Mitchell Thomas trying to recapture his form of 12 years ago, and Marvin Johnson – a trier, but a ten-year liability not worthy of a place in the side, never mind being made club captain after the sale of his iconic defensive partner Davis. Our youth team had won the South East Counties League two seasons in a row, and Lawrence deserves credit for giving the kids a chance. Yet he picked them seemingly at random – we had a staggering 15 players who wore the No 11 shirt.

The best example of inconsistency was Andre Scarlett, a 17-year-old who came off the bench after 70 minutes for his debut against Oldham. Scarlett was sensational, first forcing an Oldham player into a red-card horror tackle then setting up the first goal for Phil Gray (yes, Sunderland fans, he's still alive). In injury time, 5ft 3in Scarlett made it 2-0. At that stage, we were ready to go straight into the First Division and flounce up their table too. Scarlett's debut, said older fans, was the best since Ricky Hill's in 1976. But by the end of the season, after a few desperate starts, it was clear he wasn't ready after all and was struggling to do much for the reserves.

Similar tales could be told of at least five of his colleagues. Surely one of them will be of some use. The wage-bill cut got rid of one, Jimmy Cox, so I'm now patiently waiting for the tabloid headline reading **Third Division Luton Coxed It Up With Wenger's £8 million New Signing!** Lawrence was patently unable to inspire any confidence whatsoever, surely vital with so many nervous youngsters in the team. Trying to be popular to the veterans too meant Lawrence had landed Luton with a wage bill of £1.8 million, the fourth highest in a division which included the not-nearly-so-skint Fulham, Manchester City, Wigan, Reading, Preston and Stoke.

Paul Showler, who had played four games in two years through injury, was still on First Division wages. So was year-long casualty Julian James. Even more stupid was the sale of goalkeeper and player of the season Kelvin Davis, also to Wimbledon. The fee, £600,000, was reasonable enough. Less forgivable was that Lawrence, even though he knew Davis was on his way, gave a free transfer to his promising understudy Tanny Abbey. Luton's only remaining keeper was the youth team's 17-year-old Daniel Tate. Thankfully, Abbey's sale to Antwerp was never completed because of a problem with the paperwork. When Davis actually left, Lawrence finally realised his lack of options and cancelled Abbey's transfer.

If going into receivership had any benefit, it was that idiocies like this were finally exposed and taken note of. The problems at the club are as much to do with competence as lack of staff. It is widely accepted that there are at least a thousand stay-away fans who have given up coming to Kenilworth Road in protest at the club's administration. One example is the failure to keep fans properly informed. There have not been any cash turnstiles at Kenilworth Road since our 1980s away-fan ban – but the ticket office does sell tickets to the main stand on match days. Understandably, but mistakenly, casual fans think you cannot simply turn up on Saturday afternoon and expect to get in; a big joke among us regulars who frequently get more space to ourselves than Paul Ince at a West Ham Supporters Club party.

These are relatively minor gripes, but symptomatic of the over-stretched resources at the club and its lack of imagination in reaching out to new fan bases. We have never experimented with the kid-a-quid offers which have become commonplace at lower division clubs. More worryingly, Luton have never made any attempts to attract supporters from the area's large Asian population.

The most important and surprising result of going into receiver-ship, however, was that the fans finally came together to form their first independent supporters' association, FLAG. If the Bassett/Kohler spat was bitter, you should see the hatred among some of our own fans. I still remember the last real punch-up in the Kenny End, which was between two fans arguing over whether Kim Grant was any good. We were beating Preston 5-1 at the time.

Kohler virtually blamed Loyal Luton Supporters for inciting the letter bomb; the *Mad as a Hatter* fanzine didn't get on with the official supporters club; the fans who only went to away games said we the rest of us were suckers for turning up to Kenilworth Road, thus letting the allegedly incompetent ticket office staff get away with murder. FLAG finally seems to have solved all that nonsense. As Bassett debated whether to talk to Kohler again, the new group tried to organise the purchase of the latter's 61 per cent stake in the club.

The first public meeting raised £10,000. But it became clear we'd need backing from other businessmen, the way community-run Bournemouth do, if we were to properly take over. None were really forthcoming. At one stage during the summer it looked like we might officially become the first nursery club. Galling enough, even more so when it became clear our overlords would be the mighty Spurs. Finally, it emerged Bassett was indeed taking over. Once he and Kohler got talking, the main sticking point was over the new ground.

Kohler's sole vision during his nine-year spell was the Kohlerdome. Even though he had left, Kohler wanted to retain the ownership of the potential new ground. He claimed Luton could be rent-free tenants. Bassett and the other two directors laughed in his face and Kohler was finally paid off. While no longer sponsoring our kit and not wanting the administrative work involved in being chairman, Bassett was officially the new owner. After all, our debts were only an estimated £4.2 million. No worse than most Nationwide clubs these days, is it?

At the first home game of the 1999-2000 season, a Worthington Cup tie against Bristol Rovers, there was a party atmosphere. The programme took the piss out of Kohler, talks were resuming on a new ground and we had money to buy new players. Things were surely changing. We lost 2-0. Lennie Lawrence was still manager.

But that at least is a situation we are used to. It's rarer for the two main directors to be sulking at each other, to have a stadium cancelled by roadworks, to field a full team plus substitutes in the same position, to worry if you can afford that Sunderland reserve available on a free who looked pretty good on loan. That's a nightmare we'll be glad to put behind us. The only problem is, if we ever get to be a sane club like Bournemouth or Walsall, why do I get the twisted feeling I'll be nostalgic for the days when Luton lived in "interesting" times?

coveted perth
archie macgregor

Europe had spent 28 years wondering when St Johnstone would be coming back again. Finally, they had their answer

It was St Johnstone's finest season ever.

Thrashed 5-0 at Celtic Park. Gubbed 7-0 at home by Rangers. Manager cleared off a month into the season. Lumbering 32-year-old striker ended up as top scorer with a handsome return of six goals. And, last but not least, it turned out our biggest celebrity fan was a former drummer with the Average White Band. Like I say, season 1998-99 was the stuff of dreams.

The thing is, it really was. Out of the wreckage of this wounding embarrassment and wretched humiliation the objective measures stand up – a League Cup final appearance, Scottish Cup semi-finalists, a record-equalling third place finish in the top division and, hurrah, qualification for Europe. As well as providing a telling admission about the current condition of the Scottish game that a litany of such apparent bumbling ineptitude should not prove an impediment to success, it was also, for me, a case of at long last getting back to where we started, 28 years on.

Many a lifelong supporter has been born of an exhilarating first-time-ever-at-a-match experience. It was emphatically so for me – yet the giddy euphoria was to have a slow-burning and grim aftermath. My introduction to St Johnstone FC also transpired to be, in the words of the club's official history, their finest ever 90 minutes. It was September 29th, 1971, UEFA Cup first round, second leg: St Johnstone 3, SV Hamburg 0 (aggregate 4-2).

Of all the shameless duplicity. If it had all gone something like true to form and they had battled earnestly, only to go out to a scrappily conceded away goal... well, I might not have fallen into the trap and instead spent the best part of the past three decades having a whale of a time aboard the glory seekers express supporting Celtic or Rangers as they triumphantly obliterated all those feeble, shitey wee teams up and down Scotland season after season. What's more, I would have had half the football population of Perth for company. But no, the deception was absolute, my infatuation complete, the commitment solemnly sworn.

Naturally it was all downhill from there on. Relegations, inglorious cup exits, near bankruptcy, ground safety certificate failures, gormless managers and players galore. Nothing particularly remarkable about it either. Such, after all, is the lot of the supporter of the small- to medium-sized provincial club in Scotland. You get your 15 or maybe even 90 minutes of fame, then it's bog off, go back to being Old Firm cannon fodder again for the next 30 or 40 years. Overdosing on nostalgia is an inevitable consequence. While the Saints did go on to dispose of Vasas Budapest and beat Zeljeznicar of Sarajevo at home before being regally shafted in the return leg, nothing has quite recaptured the glow of that September evening at Muirton Park and my humbly cherished but often seemingly barely credible wish ever since has been to see them participate in European competition again.

In view of the recent record of Scottish clubs in Europe, adopting UEFA Cup qualification as your Holy Grail does seem to fall into the category of lemmings going for a stroll along the cliffs when it comes to flawed ambitions. It is not that there are a lot of fearful hammerings from the continent's elite to dwell upon – it's worse than that. In the past five years we have witnessed exits at the hands of a French second division side and Finnish, Latvian and Slovakian opposition at the first or even preliminary round stages. Dundee United's appearance in a UEFA Cup final in 1987 seems so long ago it might as well have been in a previous century.

Personally I blame the Souness revolution. The precipitous decline in Scottish clubs' fortunes coincides uncannily with the moustachioed Messiah's arrival at Ibrox. Yet no matter how questionable the goal, nor how ominous the portents, no side or its supporters is going to shy away should the prospect of European competition present itself. God knows, there are so few chances to get away from our hellish climate that any half-decent excuse to jump on a plane cannot afford to be spurned. And who knows, looking on the bright side, the whole thing might well end up with your team being roundly patronised for its plucky resistance, as Raith and Motherwell were for their honourable defeats by Bayern and Dortmund.

At the start of this season, the possibility that the hearts of some Lithuanian or Icelandic club officials might be gladdened by the announcement that they had just been paired with some bunch of obscure no-hopers called FC Perth St Johnstone in the UEFA Cup seemed as remote a prospect as it had been for just about every other of the previous 27 years. Indeed it seemed feasible that we had blown our allotted once-in-a-generation opportunity of grabbing a European place in the preceding campaign when we lost out in the race for the sole remaining UEFA Cup place to Kilmarnock on the last day of the season. It was obviously going to be the usual suspects this time around – Celtic, Rangers, the revitalised Hearts having emerged from 40 years of trophyless wilderness, and so on.

Expectations were hardly set hurtling towards the outer atmosphere when, after a handful of games, the respected, if not entirely adored, Paul Sturrock did exactly what we knew he would from the moment he walked through the door at McDiarmid Park – that is, went scurrying back down the road to his first love Dundee United when the SOS call came from his grumpy old mentor Jim McLean. When it was announced that his successor would be the Hamilton manager, Sandy Clark, it was greeted with muted acceptance. Here was a safe pair of hands who would probably maintain his predecessors' diligent endeavours without remotely threatening to break the mould of history. Sure it was slightly easier to adapt his name to the tune of the old terracing stomper "Here we go", but we're hardly talking about a cue for wild street parties.

Yet almost from the day of his arrival, the stoical folk of Perth became fixated with Europe in a manner not seen since the last EU directive on health and safety regulations for tattie pickers. It may have been Clark's good fortune that his first game in charge should be a League Cup quarter-final against Hibs, but the majestic fashion in which they and then their Edinburgh rivals Hearts were swept aside on route to the final had most of us suspecting that our half-time Bovrils had been laced with hallucinogenic substances.

In the hazy delirium nobody had bothered paying much attention to the small print which said the competition no longer granted its winners a place in Europe. Not that we ever looked like overcoming Rangers on the big day anyway. The final scoreline of 2-1 made it appear closer than it really was, with our poor guys still bearing the psychological scars of a terrible seven-goal drubbing from the Govan mob in a Sunday evening televised league match only three weeks previously. Never had *Songs of Praise* seemed such compulsive viewing.

For a support used to living with diminished expectations, a cup final appearance would in itself have been enough to ensure that season 98-99 went down in the annals as a "success". Much to our near amazement, however, the team, having seen one route to Calais and beyond severed, went in search of alternatives. Next up was the Scottish Cup. Unfortunately, having got as far as the semis we ran into an all too familiar roadblock: Rangers. Most Scottish teams have a hang-up about playing this shower – over the past decade or so even Celtic's record against them has bordered on the abysmal – but with Saints it has been more akin to a full blown allergy. Here again it was the same old story. Time for a sharp exit.

Such is the boundless, something-for-everyone spirit of generosity that sweeps through the corridors of UEFA these days that you don't have to be particularly good to get an invitation to one of their parties any more. Hell, you don't even have to be champions to win the Champions League. Among the burgeoning booby prizes for the not-so-rich and TV-audience-friendly are the Intertoto Cup and Fair Play awards.

It would be nice to think that the Saints and the rest of Scottish football collectively turned up their noses at the former out some sort of principled stand against mediocrity. In truth, it was more down to witnessing the harrowing experiences of Partick Thistle's solitary foray in the competition in 1995 when, apparently burnt out by having to take on some humble outfits from Austria, Croatia and Iceland, they ended up being relegated from the Premier League.

As for the Fair Play wild card entry, it is surely a measure of the ludicrous extremes that the European game's governing body is prepared to go in subjugating achievement on merit to near random events, that Scotland's pole position in the rankings was apparently held to be in jeopardy due to the level of whistling during the playing of the Czech national anthem prior to the Euro 2000 qualifier at Celtic Park in March. Add to this that for a long time it appeared that the worst Aberdeen team in living memory would be the grateful recipients and the notion that this was no more than UEFA's equivalent to a village fete lucky dip approaches damning proportions.

So we stumbled on to the last gasp saloon – qualification by finishing third in the league. Sure we looked on gleefully as the puffed up challenges from Hearts, Aberdeen and Dundee United quickly imploded and Saints doggedly hugged the mid-table comfort zone. But there remained one niggling yet significant doubt over our capabilities of defying the odds: Kilmarnock. On the face of it not one of the all-conquering giants of the world game, but somehow the Ayrshire side had assumed the status of our nemesis, though the two clubs have no geographical or historical basis for anything approaching a serious rivalry.

In 1994, an attritional relegation battle involving us and Killie had gone to the final game of the season, with the Rugby Parkers eventually sending us down on goal difference. Fast forward to 1998 and the greedy swine denied us a place in Europe. One year on, the curtain comes down and, yep, it's us against them again.

In such situations, the supporter's DIY guide to conspiracy theories comes into its own. No Saints fan could help but notice that in 1994 and 1998 Killie had delivered the knock-out blow by recording two totally unexpected victories over Rangers in their penultimate games. The 1994 experience left a particular bitter taste in the mouth, with our friends in Govan sending out a team so palpably weakened it even featured a centre back pairing of Oleg Kuznetzov and Mark Hateley.

And just who were Killie playing in their last game on May 16th? A Rangers team that had already won the championship. With Kilmarnock now featuring two individuals by the names of Durrant and McCoist in their ranks, it was a case of double helpings of paranoia for breakfast, dinner and tea.

The simple arithmetic was that if Kilmarnock won at Ibrox, they would get third place. Even if they drew or lost we were still out on our backsides if we failed to win our last game. Just to add another delicious irony, our match happened to be against our true derby rivals, Dundee – never forgiven for winning their one and only League championship while relegating us at the same time in 1962.

It was to be one of those occasions when, for a supporter, time and space lose their order and become amorphous blobs. For the entire game myself and thousands of others sat with headphones welded to the ear drums. We may have been sitting at McDiarmid Park, but our senses were zigzagging across the stratosphere between Perth and Glasgow at the speed of sound. At half-time, with the scores standing at 0-0 at McDiarmid and 1-1 at Ibrox, demands were being made for a FIFA enquiry as to how the referee could possibly have allowed the first half to have lasted for what seemed no more than five minutes.

To the second half. Just how did our goalkeeper Alan Main tip away a header from five yards out from Dundee's Jim Grady? Then, just how did Paul Kane manage to score for us, in turn with a header, which took about three hours to loop its way into the net? The remaining 20 minutes were spent entirely at Ibrox, with Rangers and Kilmarnock level at 1-1. Just excruciating. Stop it, stop it. Blow the bloody whistle, ref. And finally, mercifully, he did. One carefully crafted persecution complex bites the dust – we had done it. Go wild? I tell you, those Man Utd fans don't even know they have lived. Poor, wee, insignificant, nondescript St Johnstone. We had finally achieved something meaningful.

By about seven o'clock that evening the Saints were already well on their way to Europe. The string of slurred and incoherent messages left on bewildered friends' answerphones had extended as far as Germany. A crushing hangover was rapidly in the making. This, no doubt, is an only too apposite metaphor for what will happen on the field of play in the very near future.

But who cares? Winning isn't everything. Just now and again it is.

can't beat
the feeling
ivan briscoe

Argentina's season was punctuated by violence, strikes and clubs going bankrupt. Even more unusually, Boca Juniors proved unbeatable

The team's players, coaches and directors had just settled down for a consolation sleep in the mountain air of western Argentina, when a rude and angry set of voices awoke them. A small but vocal group of fans, heartily sickened by watching their side wilt in a summer holiday version of the capital's derby of derbies, were taking the matter to the team hotel. First, they called for certain players to come down and "talk". The players, only too familiar with the fans from practice ground nuttings and insinuations of untimely death, clung to their sheets without a murmur. "Clear off then," the determined group resumed, in what has become a classic stadium chant of modern Argentine football, "and don't rob any more."

It was a typical scene from an atypical season of that raucous, delirious and thoroughly grubby sport some English settlers once innocently decided to introduce to the Argentine. River Plate, the grand and silken-skilled Buenos Aires club which had just lost to its old foe Boca Juniors, had enraged its hardcore element: the *barra brava*, or wild bunch, a species common to just about every major club in the country. A week before, Boca's own version of the *barra* had imposed "justice" using wooden clubs on a hated band of rivals in front of television cameras at a friendly. Two of Boca's star players called to the bat-wielders by name and asked them to stop the thrashing. No one was too surprised by the intimacy.

Disentangling the threads which lead from the lads with the bats to the Mercedes-driving directors and the big boys in politics is not something most Argentinians seem inclined to do. Yet this year, for virtually the first time in 90 years of football, the scale of skulduggery threatened to become clear. Argentine football spent its year hanging out rotten laundry that begged for close inspection. There were fights, strikes, threats and clubs which collapsed and resurfaced with unpaid hotel bills from 1991. Players fled to Europe and the millions went somewhere oddly invisible. A beloved referee resigned, complaining of massive match-fixing, and was accused by the authorities of plotting a career in new age politics.

And above it all, led by Carlos Bianchi, a coach with a marked resemblance to an Old Testament prophet, Boca Juniors ended their six-year losing streak and began to pummel every club they met. They had the *barra*, true, but when the results went their way they also got Boca teddies, Boca annuals and Boca socks. Through all the dirt, a new era of mass merchandising was starting to glimmer, and the paying customer was king.

It was, without any shred of doubt, Boca's season. After a short, ill-starred spell managing Roma, Bianchi had returned via the World Cup commentary box to a club which had been mired in what one discontented player called "cabaret". Managers tripped on and off stage, playing strategy for the past three years had been based on whether Diego Maradona could make it to the ground without a lengthy detour and well-paid squad members had taken offence at the concept of running.

But while every other club was suffering from European suction fever – about 15 of the league's top players left in the close season, including River Plate's Marcelo Salas, for an appetising total of $75 million – Boca sold virtually no one and got serious. Bianchi implanted a firm defence, a diligent midfield, a bit of trickery and a cumbersome, blond-fringed striker called Martin Palermo with a head designed for ball contact – he would make his name around the world in July 1999 by missing three penalties in Argentina's 3-0 Copa America defeat against Colombia.

By the time the English season was drawing to a close, which in Argentine football language translates as the middle of the second mini-league of the year, Boca were still unbeaten in the league and had demolished most clubs. Palermo and his pock-marked, hip-swinging accomplice, Guillermo Barros Schelotto, were being compared by some more inebriated pundits to Di Stefano and Puskas. The two had scored a goal on average every 62 minutes. In the end Boca went 40 matches without defeat, breaking the record set by Racing in 1966, though their celebrations for winning the *clausura* championship in June were tempered by a 4-0 defeat at Independiente which ended the run.

Those with a deeper knowledge of the painful drainage of talent from Argentine grounds, however, put on a more sober face. Boca's triumphal procession, they argued, lay over several clubs in mid-atrophy. The wan defences they faced might just as well have been overwhelmed by a steady gaze. "Boca showed that by being only normal, and without needing to be a great side, they could become champions," declared Juan Zuanich of the sports newspaper *Ole*. The word "mediocrity" seemed to trip off pundits' lips.

But for the Boca faithful it made no difference. Supporting Boca, as the stadium chant would have it, is a "feeling", and aesthetics were best left to River Plate's red-striped ponces from the posh suburbs. A Boca fan, and there are many of them, is rather like a Peronist, who tends to believe that power is best in quantity and that history is what you say it is. All of a sudden, after grand victories like that over Ferro (an old railway club, whose fan base can be numbered in the tens) or

Platense (famous largely for their supporters who throw stones collected from a nearby train line), Boca were a living instance of footballing domination.

In the week leading up to match which clinched the *apertura* title in November – 90 minutes of uninterrupted, goalless boredom, ending in a firework-lit frenzy of players jumping into nets and fans sobbing with delight – television news spent a good 20 minutes each night analysing the structure and size of the queue to buy tickets. When the ticket booths opened on a day of paralysing heat, a small but good-humoured riot broke out which police answered with cooling jets of waters. The "incidents", as they were called, dominated the news, relegating the arrest of one of the country's more psychopathic former military rulers into second place, straight after an interview with the Boca fan who was first in line.

Yet, as the club's faithful are quick to point out, its fan-base is "half plus one" of the population of Argentina. It is the majority club, the obvious choice. No city in the country is free from groups of young men wearing Boca's blue and yellow home kit. And the fans themselves have turned their support into a peculiar kind of art. Go to a match at River Plate's home ground, and you will generally find yourself surrounded by mild-mannered folk who reach their highest pitch of virulence when their own players fall over the ball – 50 right hands rise up simultaneously, and a cacophonous shout of (in literal translation) "the whore that gave birth to you" is the standard response. Go to Boca, by contrast, and you form part of a 90-minute, modern-day Dionysian ritual. You sing, jump, run in circles for ages, spit at authority and dodge tear gas.

"River was collar-and-tie. Boca was overalls. River was office-workers, bureaucrats, academics. Boca was more port, more workshop, more dance-hall, more noisy," wrote one famous Boca author in 1980, and the image still sticks. Deep in the dilapidated port area of Buenos Aires, Boca's homeland is a place of dingy brothels, barbecue smells and men exposing their swollen bellies on the pavement. Though the fans come from far and wide, the "feeling" is shared: supporting Boca is in some way about communing with those early Argentinians, fresh off the boats, working in the tanneries and absolutely penniless.

Boca fans laugh at fans of River and multiple Copa Libertadores winners Independiente for being too sophisticated and stuck-up. River fans, in contrast, sing about the Boca lot – 46 per cent of whom, according to a poll in the club's annual, have only primary school education – beating their women.

Anyone with a nose for profit could have seen that Boca was an obsession waiting to be exploited. Yet, this being Argentine football, most of the club's directors until the late Nineties were only interested in furthering their political careers and recruiting a few *barra* for the odd job around election time.

Not until the arrival in 1995 of Mauricio Macri, son of a concrete magnate who emigrated as a boy from Italy, did the coffers start jingling. Scenting the way football was evolving worldwide, Macri gave Boca the corporate makeover. He roped in Nike for sponsorship, struck up a deal with the *Clarin* newspaper group to move 500 Boca products (resulting, naturally, in highly impartial media coverage of the club), and watched revenue soar.

Macri's boom was in keeping with the temper of the times. "There is almost no television programme, whatever its subject, which does not refer at one moment to football," raged the renowned Argentine sociologist Juan Jose Sebreli in a recent best-selling assault on the sport. "There are games all day, all the time, even simultaneously... There's no way to evade it, not even dissident or indifferent people can stop taking part in some way, there is no space for oneself, no worry which is not football."

But Sebreli's nemesis – football as big business – formed only the gift-wrapped side of a perturbing split personality in Argentina's season. For while Boca's squad smugly took in the summer sun after winning the first league of the season, several kinds of damnation were being visited on the sport. And it was, inevitably, *barra* violence which blew apart the lucrative love-in of football, politics and television.

Events in the first few months of 1998 – shootings of fans, 392 arrests, pitched battles in the pricy seats of a minor First Division club – prompted Victor Perrotta, a plump judge with a crucifix dangling in his office, to act. In May, he declared the first suspension of the league, instantly bringing upon him the wrath of the fans and those who line their pockets with the fans' assistance. As is customary in Argentina, a string of unfathomable pressures and illustrious cabals brought poor Perrotta to his senses, and football started again a few weeks later, just as it was, apart from a vague promise by the authorities to convert everyone to the merits of family outings to the stadium. But the family, it appeared, did not take the bait. Riots engulfed a Second Division match in December, and Perrotta wielded his trusty judicial plume once again.

This time, his suspension only affected lower league sides, but the players' union – keen to reassert their weight after at least a year without a walk-out – voted to strike in protest. By February 1999, the case had been lost in a maze of conflicting courts, players were starving through lack of wages and the cabals had called in President Menem to preserve, as he put it, "the hen that lays the golden eggs". Judge Perrotta, meanwhile, had become exasperated at the chasm separating footballing mores and the law.

"Hypocrisy and egoism abound," the judge told one newspaper. "The *barra* don't come about by themselves, they are fed and protected... When anyone has to take concerted action, they think votes."

As the judge and most journalists fully realised, the *barra* stood at the base of a pyramid which had its apex in the inner sanctums of power. One list of the top 100 *barra* – every self-respecting football journalist knows exactly who they are – showed that the lads had been mixed up in all manner of wrongdoing, from the murder and burning of a journalist to some who had joined military death-squads under the dictatorship. Their bosses are men like Luis Barrionuevo, eternal head of a union for restaurant staff, chief of the Chacarita club and, to cap it all, one of Menem's best chums and zealot for his failed re-election bid.

Their functions were various: controlling prima donna players, beefing up political rallies which would otherwise be attended by a couple of stray dogs and carrying out sundry "tasks". In return, they would get free tickets, access to halls of power and the liberty to do what they wished with a wooden bat. For the football association and television bosses – who had a $200 million monopoly to worry about – they were best left to their arcane rituals. No surprise, then, that Perrotta let the case slip gently away.

Yet fractures in the devilish *barra* alliance had started to show at both River and Boca. The new world of juicy transfer fees and television revenue sloshing from one account to another had left the old scheming out in the cold. Now club directors had more important matters to attend to with their accountants. Now the *barra* were reduced to congregating outside pleasant mountain hotels to plead: "... and don't rob any more".

Victims of the changing ways in Argentine football were many. Those smaller clubs which make up the typical cannon fodder on a Sunday afternoon had been earmarked by the tyrant of televised football, Carlos Avila, as ripe for enforced relegation. A referee known as "the sheriff" for his by-the-book ways had left the services of the Argentine FA for good after hinting at uncontrollable match-fixing in the interests of the mighty few. And above all else, one of the nation's greatest clubs – the very first Argentine one to win the World Club Championship through a well-struck left foot shot against Celtic in 1967 – went bankrupt, was told to close, was told to re-open and then kept on losing as before.

Racing Club, based out in the monoblock suburbs of Buenos Aires, had mounted up some grand debts in its 32-year streak of winning absolutely nothing. A complete set of the *Encyclopaedia Britannica*, unpaid for, sat in the club library. One Uruguayan player was still waiting for his fees from 1981, while hotels, bus companies and some 355 creditors were clawing desperately for their cash. In total, club debts were estimated to stand at around $62 million, and the club was still haemorrhaging more.

The basic problem for Racing and, in truth, for every club apart from

Boca and River, is that poor performances erode attendances to a quite breathtaking extent. Images of fluttering scraps of paper and palpitating crowds crammed into Argentine stadiums are all very nice, but a mid-season trip to Racing's hauntingly large ground would usually reveal a crowd numbering in the hundreds, forlonly hugging a few grilled sausage stalls.

Naturally, the news in early March that the club faced imminent closure uncorked that ever-bubbling "feeling". Racing's fans, an emotional breed at the best of times, took to the streets to wring their wetted handkerchiefs and sing the old tunes. "With all the problems you have to live with in this shitty country, now they have to go and close Racing," moaned one disgusted fan. Club president Daniel Lalin went before a group of enraged fans to insist that it would all turn out all right, but his assurances failed to have the desired effect: "Baldy", as Lalin is known, was rudely clipped over the eye by an accurately thrown drum.

Only days later, with Racing banned from playing the first match of the season, 35,000 – well above the normal crowd – congregated in the stadium to mark the greatness of their mourning. Days later, after the cabals had done their job and issued the right threats, the judge who ordered the closure explained that he had, in fact, not done so at all. Play resumed, and Racing, in keeping with tradition, lost their first match 2-1.

Within weeks came fresh closure orders, yet more protests were carried out (including the thrashing of five watching journalists) and the stench of surefire club death gently rose. Club directors took the most effective measure they could conceive, ordering players to bring their own food to the hotel before an away match. Unused encyclopaedia obviously offered little nourishment.

"Everyone has to allow themselves to be dragged by the whirlwind of footballing passion, or be destroyed by it," decries Sebreli in his diatribe on the "totalitarian" sport. For Julio Grondona, the man who has presided over the Argentine Football Association during the last 20 years with notorious phlegm, the season's "whirlwind" could not have been easy. Still, here is a man who survived Maradona's epic drug fiascos, and his stamina appears undimmed. Legend has it that a ring on his left hand bears a simple inscription: *Todo pasa.* Or, in very rough translation: "Shit happens."

fan and semi-fan
mike ticher

Some clubs increasingly know the price of everything and the value of nothing. Chelsea may well be one of them

The 1998-99 season began early for me, on February 16th to be precise. It was the day Chelsea announced their season-ticket prices. The previous year mine had cost £435. Now the price for renewals rose to £525 (a year later it would go up again, to £595). Payment by the end of April, please, in full.

I didn't take me long to decide against it. For a start, I didn't have £525. And kids (a second one due in the summer) increasingly made demands on my weekend time. But what brought me up short was that I no longer felt I really belonged there. Nor, even more surprisingly, did I really want to.

I knew that failing to renew would mean going to far fewer matches. Tickets for individual league matches went on sale in three blocks. In August, when the second set of six went on sale, a friend who had also given up their season ticket rang up. Did I want to go to any of the games up to and including Southampton at home on February 6th? And if so, could I get £138 to them within the week, please?

Somewhere back there I'd crossed a line marking off a world where this sort of thing seemed like a reasonable way of organising your life and one in which I frankly could not be bothered to make the effort. Once inside the ground I can feel as involved and committed as the next person. But missing the match does not hurt in the way it once did. Disentangling the reasons why was less simple, but three factors emerged as the season unfolded.

The first was to do with the way the football boom has changed the relationship between bigger clubs and their supporters. Looking back at the end of the season, I would have liked to have seen more games than the dozen or so I eventually mustered. But on the other hand, I had no sense of disloyalty. Fifteen or so years ago I used to worry about the size of the crowd. Was it going up or down? How did we compare with West Ham? Empty spaces on the terraces made me depressed. Now, the attendance figure is the same for every league game, give or take a few hundred. If I don't go, someone else, probably thousands of people, will be only too glad to pay £25 and more for my seat.

It's not that in the past you went out of a sense of duty, exactly. But there was a definite feeling of cussedness (or self-righteousness) about being there when so many stayed away. And besides, if people stopped going, it encouraged the people who wanted to knock the stadium down and build flats on it, not to mention the politicians, journalists and others who thought football as a whole should be shut down.

So it was a two-way thing: football gave you pleasure (perhaps) and you gave it money, time, angst and moral support. The fundamental irrationality of investing your hopes and fears in a random and ever-changing collection of players seemed then like a given – a natural state of affairs that would continue for ever. Unlike music, you were never expected to "grow out of" football, but to grow old with it and pass it on until you found yourself boring your grandchildren with stories of how it only cost 50p to get in to see Tommy Langley fall over his feet.

Now this thread is breaking, a process which leaves me disorientated, but which seems irreversible. To be a fan you have to leave rational thought to one side, at least for the 90 minutes. Once you start questioning the basis of your support for a club and allow logic to enter the equation the whole thing can quickly start to unravel.

Fans have always been treated badly by their clubs, not least at Chelsea. But for me it is only since they have treated me as a consumer that I have begun to behave like one. That is, to behave as if I have a choice. Is this, or is this not, how I want to spend my Saturday afternoons? Not to mention occasional Sunday mornings and, increasingly, my Monday, Tuesday, Wednesday and even Thursday nights? The club, and the game itself, no longer need me. In fact, if they were honest, they would much rather have someone with a bit more cash. The unmistakable message from Chelsea in particular – that the true fan is the one who spends the most money at the club – was the second cause of my disaffection.

In February, Ken Bates gave evidence in the case brought by the Office of Fair Trading over the Premier League's right to sell television rights collectively. Asked whether there were people who couldn't afford to watch Chelsea on a regular basis, he said: "No, I would disagree. The fact of the matter is that they can afford it, they just can't get the tickets. There is a minority too poor to come to Chelsea, but they are such a minority I don't think it's worth taking into consideration."

In one sense, of course, Bates is right. Chelsea do not lose out because their tickets are priced beyond the means of supporters. The demand is such that they can ratchet up the price every year and, so far, still fill the ground every week. For most seats they offer no concessions for children or OAPs (another sure-fire way to break the link between generations of fans) and that seems to make a certain kind of business sense, albeit an extremely short-sighted one.

But the fact is there are many people who would like to watch more often but who cannot afford to do so. Or, perhaps more accurately, cannot justify the amount of money it costs, to themselves or their families. And amazingly, even though I earn somewhere close to the average wage, I find I'm now one of them.

Chelsea may not think those people are "worth taking into consideration", but other clubs still do. Shortly after booking my tickets for the February matches (that's back in August, remember) I was enviously comparing notes with a Middlesbrough fan. At Boro, he told me, season tickets cost around £250-£300, and you could pay in instalments throughout the season. They put aside a block of seats for unemployed people. He is a member of Middlesbrough Supporters South, who get a regular supply of tickets, due in part, he said, to their support of the club in the grim days of the old Third Division. He told me how, due to a mix-up, MSS weren't allocated any tickets for the 1997 FA Cup final. Boro's chairman Steve Gibson rang up the MSS chairman to apologise, and the club chased around to rustle up as many tickets as they could for them.

I try to imagine Ken Bates doing the same, but all I can think of are the newspaper stories accusing Chelsea of breaking FA regulations by selling tickets for the same match as part of a corporate package. There are hundreds of small ways a club can send messages to its supporters. And, as the Middlesbrough example shows, they have needed to lean on the very core of their fanbase when times are tough. Most clubs, with Chelsea in the forefront, are gambling that such times will never come again.

The next step is a "loyalty scheme" which will help determine who has priority for tickets for Cup finals and other big matches. Every time you buy tickets (and in future probably also merchandise from the megastore) a swipe card records the amount and awards you points which push you further up the list.

To be a true Chelsea fan in 1999 you should take out your house-hold and motor insurance with them ("I have saved money using Chelsea Insurance and I know of many others who have also benefited," says a Mr K Bates of London SW6), join the Chelsea Racing Club ("a ridiculously low cost of £200") and dine frequently at Canaletto's, Fishnets, the Kings Brasserie and Arkles, the fantastically pompous upmarket theme restaurants that now litter Stamford Bridge. All this is alienating enough, and with every invitation that dropped through the letterbox to win a sports car by answering a lifestyle questionnaire

("Would you or your spouse consider investing £25,000 or more through a Portfolio Management Service?") I felt more justified in letting the club drift out of my life.

What made it even easier was the third factor – a wider feeling of distaste for the obsessional behaviour that football has come to indulge. At the end of September there was a TV documentary on Alex Ferguson. Stuart Kennedy, the former Aberdeen full-back, recalled how Ferguson would tell the players he worked so hard that he hadn't seen his kids grow up. "And that's how I want you to be too," he insisted. Ferguson's wife Cathy explained how she tried to remind him that there are things other than football when he comes home. His response is: "Well, maybe, but try telling the fans that."

Ferguson is driven by his own personality to work 18 hours a day, travelling incessantly to watch matches and poring relentlessly over football videos. For all his undoubted qualities, this is the lifestyle of a warped and truncated man. The fans make him a hero for it when he wins trophies, but blaming their demand for success seems to me a poor excuse. In May, as the title race came to a climax, a newspaper profile of Arsène Wenger revealed similar traits. "He occasionally visits his girlfriend and their two-year-old daughter in the south of France," we learn. But on the whole he prefers to stay up until the early hours with the video machine too. And in his leisure time? "I watch football."

Chelsea have their own standard-bearer for this approach. In Channel 4's documentary on the travails of their youth team a couple of years ago, Graham Rix's "motivational" bullying of his charges drummed into them the fact that "if football isn't the most important thing in your life, then you're no good to me". This season, the club's reaction to Rix's conviction for having under-age sex was to minimise the serious-ness of the offence and imply that the girl and her family shared much of the blame. And so he was welcomed back – whatever happens, nothing can be allowed to stand in the way of the football.

Of course, a fan going to a match every week does not compare with the degree of tunnel vision exhibited by someone at the top of the managerial or coaching profession. And lots of people who do devote large parts of their life to it can keep it all in perspective. But the cult of obsession has been lovingly nurtured in the football boom years. Now that Sky broadcast live matches almost every night of the week, you can all but live your life inside the bubble of planet football, and no one in there is going to tell you that even the most tediously completist mindset is socially unacceptable.

There comes a point – and the time when you have young children is an obvious one – when stepping off the treadmill seems saner. True, there will still be a dull ache of absence on Saturday afternoons. But for all that football and Chelsea have played a big part in my life, the idea that you are nothing without them struck me increasingly as pathetic the longer the season went on.

The odd thing is that I switched off during one of the club's most successful seasons. Obviously I'm in a minority here, but in a way that was part of the problem. All but the most blinkered fan of a smaller club can see an element of the ridiculous in their devotion, but success breeds delusions of grandeur among fans and the club's management alike. The better we do, the more the club comes to regard itself as one of the English – and, increasingly, European – elite, with all the nauseating self-congratulation that entails.

Writing in the programme for the game against Man Utd in December, Chelsea's managing director Colin Hutchinson decreed that the clubs competing in Europe should have the option to pull out of the Worthington Cup, which would soon have to be finished by Christmas anyway; the season should be extended by two weeks at beginning and end to allow a winter break; and "even the proud tradition of the Cup might have to suffer". That is, replays should go. Oh, and UEFA need to bring in a preliminary competition to eliminate some of the "no-hopers" from national team qualifying tournaments. "It is time for some vision and radical action," he concluded ringingly.

He's entitled to his opinion, though the fact that Chelsea have always led the resistance to reducing the number of teams in the Premier League makes his pleas for a less cluttered calendar seem somewhat odd. But what really sets my teeth on edge is the attempt to implicate the fans in this egotistical fantasy. This comes with the invitation to renew my club membership in April – surely the only such letter in the country that begins: "Somebody once said that the working class is its own worse [sic] enemy."

Here Bates calls on Chelsea fans to get behind the team's drive to the top. "At Stamford Bridge our ambition is to be part of the European elite. We can only achieve that ambition if you are part of it." And how do you play your part? "The only answer is by working harder and persuading you the fans to use Chelsea's other facilities and services which you would spend money on elsewhere [sic], so please spend with us. If you want a continuous flow of great football and success, then you have to play your part – yes you – not the guy sitting next to you." Without pausing for breath he comes to point: "Do you have a Chelsea Credit Card?"

As it happens, I don't have a credit card at all, which probably reflects my own pitiful lack of ambition, but there you go. If I did get one, I'd rather get it from the conventional band of usurers rather than someone who loses no opportunity to lecture me about the failings of the working class.

When I think about what I would have liked from my club this season, qualification for the Champions League is not high on the list. In fact it's not on the list at all. I would have liked the ongoing ground development to include some reference to the club's history other than plastic tea-bars called "McCreadies". After all, museums can make money too. (There is one planned, but, typically, the club has thrown away all its memorabilia.)

I would have liked it to include some of the sporting facilities for the local community that were endlessly promised in almost every one of the bewildering number of plans for the new stadium in the Eighties. Instead of which, Ken Bates has expended his energy savaging the local residents for their opposition to the ever-changing raft of additional facilities (nightclub and cinema the last time I heard) which has prevented completion of the West Stand.

I would have liked it not to end with the summary removal of Ruth

Harding as patron of the club and the withdrawal of her seat in the directors' box. And I certainly could have done without the week in July when Andy Myers, Eddie Newton and Michael Duberry all left the club, severing almost the last links between the first team squad and the youth set-up. You can hardly argue that their replacements do not improve the squad, of course. But what I really wanted was some hint that the club is something – anything – but an empty shell housing some wonderful players.

Part of me cannot stop being a Chelsea fan, but I reserve the right to draw the line somewhere. The virtues of fandom, accepting everything football throws at you with a shrug and an appeal to your "helpless addiction", are no longer so obvious. In particular, giving huge amounts of my money to a club so rich, so mean-spirited and so contemptuous no longer seems a necessity, though I'll continue to do it from time to time.

One thing I won't be paying for is the popular line of merchandise with the slogan "Chelsea is life". It really isn't.

living next door to alex

harry golightly

A promotion season inspired by the Third Division's best-known Spaniard had some surprising effects, not least on the street names in Scunthorpe

"The people of Scunthorpe, they have been so kind and have made me and my girlfriend so welcome and happy, and now I have done something to make them happy too. I will play for this club for a very long time."

Whether or not Alex Calvo-Garcia's prediction comes true, something changed in Scunthorpe when he swooped to head the Wembley goal in May that took the town's team, perpetual underachievers and consistent play-off fall-guys, to the Second Division for the first time in 15 years.

Unable to secure a new contract with Real Sociedad, the Spanish midfielder had expressed an interest in moving abroad in 1996. His agent duly obliged by setting up a dream trial in Scunthorpe. Garcia set down his suitcases in the town with a sparse grasp of the English language and, doubtlessly, a shocked system. Inward-looking Scunthorpe is hardly a hot-bed of cultural activity, the current United manager Brian Laws memorably going so far as to call it a "scratch-off-and-sniff" sort of town. It's not grim, and at least it's not Grimsby, but it can be a grey, grey, grey place. Garcia found his new north Lincolnshire employers doing no more than ticking over in the basement division, somehow still basking in the warped glory of their penalty shoot-out defeat in the 1992 play-off final against Blackpool.

Under the old-school managership of one of the game's dourest characters, Mick Buxton, Garcia stayed but never flourished. Too often in and out of the side, he almost always seemed in danger of succumbing to the loud hum of inertia which characterised the club's progress. Many good players had passed through its doors over the years, and all gave sterling service, but all truly blossomed elsewhere.

Garcia persisted, and his determination not to let the many obstacles that stood in his way did him credit. Not for him the Premiership luxury of expensive assistants and interpreters. He enrolled in a couple of night-classes at a local tech, and his girlfriend got a job as a doctor's receptionist. The pair integrated themselves into the local community with an earnest attitude and a willingness to fit in. They seemed in Scunthorpe to settle. "He definitely didn't come here for the money, and isn't that refreshing?" commented Brian Laws.

When Laws took over as manager, many fans viewed his appointment with an overly cynical eye – this was an ex-manager of Grimsby Town, Scunthorpe's biggest rivals, and a man for whom the word "volatile" seemed to have been specially created. How could a man uniquely qualified in the art of duffing up underachieving players possibly keep up with the workload he would find at Scunthorpe United?

Whatever his techniques, and duffing up players would surely not really be one of them following the financial repercussions of the most infamous of dressing room outbursts at Grimsby, the players responded almost immediately. Scunthorpe missed out on the play-offs by one point in 1998 and indulged in a modest but encouraging amount of transfer activity during the summer.

The solid and dependable central defender Chris Hope continued to be solid and dependable, but those around him pulled their socks up to somewhere around the ears, and United became not just the team you wanted to watch out of habit and loyalty, but the team you wanted to watch because they played bloody good football.

Laws, displaying more faith in Garcia, gave him a regular place on the teamsheet and he began to shine, scoring terrific goals. It was during a stalemate against future play-off final opponents Leyton Orient that Garcia demonstrated the supposedly British characteristics of grit and determination, forcing his way through a tight and physical defence to squeeze in an important goal, one on which Laws generously commented: "He doesn't play like a foreigner."

To another stunning Garcia goal, a volley from outside the box, Laws responded: "I've been winding him up all season that he won't score from outside the box, and that if he did I'd show my backside in town. I think that's what he's asking me to do." Of course, Laws squirmed out of his cheek-baring promise, choosing instead to hide behind the borough council's decision to name a street in the town after the player. "I think that's more the sort of reward Alex deserves," said Laws, probably chortling with relief.

The bureaucrats' decision to offer the town a Garcia Way may seem strange and, let's be frank, a bit 1970s, to an outsider. But such is the affection and gratitude of the people of the town to the 27-year-old Spaniard that I can envisage even part-time supporters considering selling up their family home just to move to the newly christened thoroughfare: "Pack me Sta-Prest Sharon, we're off."

Generally, the mindset of much of the tea-drinking population of the town is one of Kafka-esque constriction. We know a whole wide world exists outside the borough's boundaries but, y'know... We fear change almost as much as we fear cappuccino. Just occasionally we are dragged into the present, and Garcia's Wembley winner has been the catalyst for for just that – Scunthorpe has been pulled kicking and screaming into a state of mind where we almost believe almost anything is possible.

There has been a dangerous outbreak of optimism around both club and town. Supporters believe the club can survive in the Second Division – and possibly go further – and the much mulled-over shopping centre redevelopment has finally been given the green light in a devil-may-care moment of brazen progressiveness.

Doubtless the councillor who signed on the dotted line is currently locked in his office, mopping his brow in a fevered burst of "Dear god, what have I done?" apprehension. Why? Because he knows the bubble may well burst some time over the next year. United may be relegated and we may find ourselves once again with our heads bowed.

But we lived off a play-off final defeat for seven years, so we'll be living off this victory for many more, whatever happens. We are sure to be cold and miserable and grey, grey, grey again one day, but we will always be able to remember a modest little Spaniard running his socks off at Wembley, and nodding the town into the present. Even if the present only lasted for a moment.

gnome defeat
ian plenderleith

For the scruffy, underdog half of Zürich
(yes, there is one), victory over Celtic
wasn't half as satisfying as a last-minute
winner from a Burundian asylum-seeker

One city, two teams. It's the same old story in Glasgow, Milan, Madrid and Manchester, cities whose identities are propped up by the symbiotic hatred of their football cultures. If you meet a Liverpudlian or a Roman in any part of the world you'll ask them: "Which side are you on?" Meet someone from Zürich and you'll likely ask: "So which bank do you work for? And where do you go skiing in winter?"

Not many people from outside Switzerland are even aware that Zürich is a city boasting two professional football clubs. Within the country the view is that the two teams, with their average home crowds of between 7,000 and 9,000, would, if they had any sense, simply merge.

Yet that would mean ignoring the century-old traditions of both and the entirely different natures of the two sides fighting to be No 1 in both city and country. Furthermore, it would mean trampling on the sentiments of the people in Zürich to whom football actually means something beyond the possible execution of a cold but financially logical alliance of resources.

The rivalry between Football Club Zürich (FCZ) and Grasshopper Club Zürich (GC) also serves to illustrate the dilemma facing clubs in second-tier footballing nations across Europe. Are we just a football club which plays to win, holding faith that values like honour, loyalty and team spirit may eventually bring their own reward (FCZ – hurrah!)? Or do we have ideas above our station? That is, do we think we can mix it with the cream of Europe? Or, put another way, can we scramble into the Champions League, make a pot of cash and patronise the rest of the clubs in the Swiss league (GC – boo!)? Reduced to a cliche which is nonetheless broadly accurate, it's the proles versus the aristocrats in terms of fans, ideals and aspirations.

Nine hundred metres, the main railway line and a philosophical crater separate the two teams. FC Zürich play in the queerly crooked Letzigrund athletics stadium, only filled to capacity for the international athletics meeting each summer. Their fans are drawn from the nearby tower blocks, Italian immigrants from the industrial suburbs and the sub-culturally hip Langstrasse area behind the main station, dwindling in numbers over the barren past two decades since the successful Sixties and Seventies.

"We played Liverpool and Real Madrid in the European Cup semi-finals," they will tell you. They may even dream that it will happen again, but they know it won't. They are bankrolled by a rich president, Sven Hotz, who by good luck is so hopelessly in love with the club he doesn't seem to mind chucking francs at his hobby.

Across the tracks, to use the local media parlance, the Grasshoppers play host at the increasingly smart Hardturm, a "proper" stand-alone football stadium which will supposedly be developed further over the coming years and may eventually accommodate both sides.

The FCZ fans delight in singing at derbies: "*GC, GC, die Scheisse vom See*" (the scum from the lake).The Grasshoppers fans do not have the wit to sing anything insulting in return. This is because they are either too young, drawn by the success of all the titles GC have accumu-

lated over the past few years, or because they are too respectable –
smartly dressed men with mobiles who do not float on top of the lake
but may well live alongside it.

The Grasshoppers view the Swiss league as a minor inconvenience
on their way to becoming Bayern Munich. They became the first Swiss
club to go public and president Romano Spadaro has made clear his
admiration for the money-generating skills on display at Old Trafford.
Each year, reaching the group stage of the Champions League is
announced as an imperative.

However, as their hopeless showing against Galatasaray proved in
this season's qualifying round, such a goal is becoming increasingly
difficult to achieve and will prove even more so in the future as Spanish,
German and Italian fourth-placed "champions" are granted access to
club football's cash cow. No wonder GC's backer and banker, Werner
Spross, got fed up in mid-season and told the public that the club is
16 million francs in debt.

It was not just the debts, the transparent arrogance and the in-fighting
centred around GC's devious director of sport, Erich Vogel, which
made it such an enjoyable first half of the season for FCZ fans.
Grasshoppers managed to get knocked out of Europe no less than
three times as well.

First, they lost to Galatasaray and missed out on the longed-for Euro-
millions. Then, after creeping past a spineless Anderlecht in the UEFA
Cup, they were 4-1 down on aggregate to Fiorentina in Salernitana (the
game having been moved because of previous crowd trouble involving
the Florence club's fans) before a fortuitous firework thrown by a
Sicilian fan caused the abandonment of the second leg at half-time
and GC took the tie. So in the next round they went out to Bordeaux
instead. Given that the home fans were outnumbered and outsung in
their own stadium against both Galatasaray and Fiorentina, it seemed
the least they deserved.

Meanwhile, FCZ had qualified for the UEFA Cup for the first time
since the early 1980s. And while the Grasshoppers cranked up ticket
prices six- or seven-fold for the Galatasaray game, Sven Hotz announced

before FCZ's qualifying round tie against the Ukrainians of Shaktyor Donetsk: "Come and watch European football at Swiss league prices." Not many did, but FCZ's cheap assemblage of Brazilians, Italian-Swiss youth, newly signed South African striker Shaun Bartlett and even a couple of Zürichers, won 4-0. They triumphed by the same scoreline against Anorthosis Famagusta in the next round and put four past Celtic too, by which time the Letzigrund was almost full and singing the cinder off the athletics track on cold, rainy, gloriously floodlit autumn evenings.

"I won't make any money out of this unless we get an Italian club in the next round," said Hotz stoically. He got his wish, and although they were narrowly eliminated, 3-2 on aggregate by Roma, everyone seemed happy. After all, they'd just beaten the Grasshoppers for only the third time since 1987. At the Christmas break, Switzerland's arcane league system decrees that the top eight of the 12 teams in the First Division have their points halved and "qualify" for the right to play each other again in the second half of the season. By this point the two teams were equal on points in second place.

From the start of the season there had been sniping between the two clubs. Grasshoppers striker Patrick de Napoli, who had been on loan with Aarau, went to train with FC Zürich and announced that he would never play for Grasshoppers again. After milking the applause of the FCZ fans at a home game before he was licensed to play, he took the time to read his contract properly and went skulking back to the Hardturm, afraid that GC would realise their threat to stop him playing at all.

Then Grasshoppers announced that their new shirt sponsors would be the private television channel Tele24. Nothing remarkable about that, except that Tele24 had for weeks been negotiating with FCZ, who were then left without a shirt sponsor for months to come (not that they needed to worry about it too much, given the pitiful quality of Tele24's output).

Finally, the two sides were forced to share the Letzigrund after the Hardturm's pitch cut up so badly it had to be completely relaid. GC's home gates tumbled as many fans refused to enter the Letzigrund on principle, even to watch their own side. And after the 2-0 home-leg defeat against Fiorentina, FCZ players taunted their counterparts from the Hardturm across the training ground.

Which set the scene nicely for the season's second derby at the Letzigrund in November. The first had been a lacklustre 0-0 draw in the stifling August sun when many fans had sensibly opted to stay by the lake. The football in the second game was not much better, but there was bite and there were goals.

FCZ took the lead through the diminutive terrace favourite Freddy Chassot before the "traitor" De Napoli equalised. Towards the end the fire began to leave the game, though, despite the dismissal of midfielder Toni Esposito, GC were the better side. Then in the 92nd minute an FC Zürich corner was pinged into a crowded penalty area, and Burundian asylum-seeker David Opango threw himself into FCZ folklore with a diving header that won the match.

"We played shit and won," beamed one FCZ supporter, "just like they've been doing to us for years."

Nothing, apparently, could go wrong for the rejuvenated FCZ. Except for the two and half month long winter break. When they came back in spring they looked as though they had spent the winter off-piste and promptly lost their first four games. One of these was at home to the Grasshoppers, where it was back to the old story of hitting the woodwork three times and losing 1-0.

Then they lost at home to Lugano in the cup in front of 1,800 fans, virtually killing off their last chance of gaining a UEFA Cup place the following season. Lugano went out in the next round to local amateur club Red Star Zürich, prompting mockers to label FCZ "Zürich's third team".

The Grasshoppers, meanwhile, had dismissed Rolf Fringer as coach. They said it was because he had failed to take GC to the Champions League group stage, although they kindly waited until Christmas to serve him with his notice. They took on St Gallen's Roger Hegi in his place, who promptly sacked a number of players. Among them was the Swiss league's only player of genuine world class, Kubilay Turkyilmaz, who took his arm-waving histrionics and dossier of injuries off to second division Locarno. For a while it worked and GC looked, as usual, the likely champions.

FCZ then remembered how to play football and closed the gap – at one stage 13 points – to just four, with three games to play, the first of them the final derby of the season in the Hardturm. Amid unprecedented enthusiasm, the 17,000 capacity ground sold out and some fans were actually locked outside. Even more unusually, FCZ outplayed the home side and won with two goals from Shaun Bartlett, while their fans took the pleasure of outchanting their rivals like it was a European tie. It was an afternoon when you realised that even in Switzerland football could be as it should be – a stadium full with people displaying extreme and irrational emotions while the peasants stuffed it up the lords.

So it was that with two games to go, there were four teams still in the running – the two Zürich sides, Lausanne the leaders, and Servette. FCZ, having worked themselves into an outside chance of winning the title, promptly lost 1-0 at home to Lausanne. Grasshoppers and Servette both won, and FCZ were out of the running. On the last day of the season, a spectacular hat-trick by the Dutchman Ed Vurens for Servette in a compelling 5-2 win at Lausanne secured the title for the team from Geneva.

Grasshoppers won 5-0 in a three-quarters empty stadium (most of the fans had school the next morning). They finished with the same number of points as Servette, more goals and a better goal difference, but were undone by the obscure league format – Servette were champions because they carried more points forward from the pre-Christmas qualification.

There was no doubt which Zürich club was left happier by that outcome. Second-placed Grasshoppers had a place in the UEFA Cup and the Swiss Cup final, but no prospect of the Champions League and its fat cheques for at least another 15 months. Fourth-placed FCZ, thanks to the Swiss Cup final being contested by Lausanne and GC, also sneaked into a UEFA Cup place, and their fans could sing "We lost GC the title" thanks to their two derby victories.

In a city where money is everything, it was possible, for just one night, to hear above the ringing of mobile phones an echo of laughter from the Letzigrund.

monopoly money

patrick harverson

One of the most significant and
surprising events of the season was the
rejection of BSkyB's bid to buy
Manchester United

Season 1998-99 may have brought Manchester United
unimaginable footballing riches, but off the field the
club suffered arguably the biggest defeat in its 121-year
history. The Department of Trade and Industry's decision to block the
proposed £623 million takeover of the club by British Sky Broadcasting
was a huge setback for the business managers at United who had
defended the deal against a well-organised campaign to keep Rupert
Murdoch's hands off football's most storied club. As unwelcome as
the comparison may be, United's shock failure to clinch the deal with
BSkyB was the business equivalent of giving up two goals in the final
three minutes of a European Cup final.

Until the government delivered its verdict on April 9th, success
seemed well within the bid proponents' grasp. From the day the takeover
offer was revealed in September 1998, most observers expected it to
be approved by the regulatory authorities, though possibly with some
conditions attached relating to the conduct of TV rights negotiations.

Stockbroking analysts in the City believed the deal would be passed, as did most competition lawyers, the club itself, BSkyB, their highly-paid PR advisers and most journalists (including me). Manchester United was a publicly-quoted company and BSkyB was another, which had offered a handsome price for its target. The two businesses were not competitors and thus it did not appear that their union would be deemed harmful to the public interest.

Both parties to the deal argued there was a powerful and persuasive commercial logic to the takeover. Yet in spite of all the talk of the mutual benefits the two would enjoy, it was clear from the start that BSkyB needed United more than United needed BSkyB. The takeover was essentially a defensive move by BSkyB, a rare display of weakness by a Murdoch-controlled company. The TV group was faced with the prospect of losing the exclusive rights to Premier League football under two possible scenarios, both unwelcome.

The first involved the possibility that the High Court might agree with the Office of Fair Trading that the BSkyB-Premier League deal was an illegal contract negotiated by 20 clubs acting as a cartel. At the time of the announcement of the United takeover, the court was preparing to hear the OFT's case and BSkyB knew that if the OFT ultimately won, its contract with the Premiership would be declared null and void. That would leave the way open for clubs to strike their own individual deals with broadcasters, destroying at a stroke BSkyB's stranglehold over domestic live football.

Buying Manchester United was a hedge against such an outcome. It also offered insurance against the second scenario – that of BSkyB losing its exclusive rights when the deal came to be renegotiated in 2000-01. The Premier League was known to be considering a new structure for its TV deals once the BSkyB contract expired, and the satellite group feared it would lose out as the League "unbundled" its rights to allow a wide range of broadcasters – terrestrial, cable, satellite and digital – to share coverage of top-flight football. As expensive as United seemed at £623 million (a figure that made the club the most valuable sports franchise in the world), to BSkyB the price was well worth paying if it meant protecting its position as English football's top broadcaster.

In contrast to the compelling business case for BSkyB's purchase of United, the case for the club accepting the offer was never that convincing. In the official Stock Exchange document sent to United shareholders in the autumn of 1998 outlining why they should accept the bid, the reasons the club gave took up all of a couple of paragraphs. Unwilling to admit that the main reason for doing so was simply because it was too good a price to turn down, the club talked about how the takeover would allow it to benefit from BSkyB's renowned sports marketing expertise. But, asked the bid's opponents, when did Manchester United, the acknowledged masters of milking football's marketing dollar, ever need help with selling itself to the world?

Later in the bid battle, United further justified the deal by talking of the substantial additional capital the club would have access to as part of the BSkyB group. This from a club that had £30 million-plus in spare cash burning a hole in its back pocket. Certainly, BSkyB could have given United another £70 million or so to outspend European competitors such as Lazio, Inter and Real Madrid, but would that have benefited the club in the long-term? Paris St-Germain have enjoyed access to the millions of its huge media group owner Canal Plus for years, but a fat lot of good it has done the woefully underperforming French club.

During the second half of the Nineties that other well-known media-owned club, AC Milan, endured a series of disappointing seasons that culminated in missing out on qualification for European competition three years in a row. Media money clearly let down the Milanese, so why should it transform United into Europe's most successful club? (With perfect ironic timing, United became just that a few months after its independent status was secured by government decree.)

There was also an argument to be made that having access to near the limitless funds of a wealthy corporate owner would actually harm, rather than help, a club like United. Football is in the grip of fierce player wage inflation, and it is the clubs which spend wisely and nurture their own talent, as United have for most of the Nineties, which will prosper in the long-term, rather than those which spend money as though it's going out of fashion – Real Madrid are in debt to the tune of at least £70 million.

These and other points were made by the various groups which opposed the BSkyB deal. Part of their case rested on an instinctive dislike of Rupert Murdoch and a deep-rooted suspicion of his motives. A hint of what life for football fans would be like with a Murdoch-controlled United was evident in the reaction of the *Sun* and the *Times* the day after the takeover bid was announced. The *Sun* wrote of how the deal had been welcomed from all quarters (B-list celebrity fans were wheeled out to give it the thumbs up) under the headline **Skyly Delighted**. The substantial fan opposition to the deal was largely ignored. Meanwhile, the chief football writer of the *Times* wrote a highly favourable piece comparing United fans to winners of the national lottery.

Murdoch papers ruthlessly promote his business interests at every possible opportunity, so the prospect of him controlling the country's biggest football club provoked fears that sports reporters' impartiality would disappear out the back window in similar fashion. Aside from these concerns, the opposition led by the formidable Shareholders United Against Murdoch group and the Independent Manchester United Supporters Association focused on issues of sporting and commercial principle.

They questioned whether the club should be allowed to fall into the hands of media industry owners whose commercial interests would always take precedence over those of the club, its supporters and the local community. Was it right that football's dominant broadcaster should own football's dominant club? Would BSkyB gain an unfair advantage in future TV rights negotiations from its ownership of the Premier League's wealthiest member?

It was that last question which, more than anything, brought the takeover deal down. A few months after the bid was blocked, a member of the Monopolies and Mergers Commission team which reported to the DTI on the offer spoke publicly for the first time. He said the deal was rejected because the undertakings given by United and BSkyB – undertakings designed to ensure the media group did not gain an unfair advantage during TV negotiations – were simply unworkable.

Even more damning was his comment that United and BSkyB could not be trusted to play fair during TV talks. "It was stretching credibility to expect parties of this nature to completely abstain [from TV negotiations]," he said. "Probably it would have worked on a nod and a wink and while it might not have breached the undertakings, it would have circumvented them."

Even if they had not done so, simple economics suggested that BSkyB could have always outbid its rivals in TV negotiations because it would have known that some of the money it paid out to the Premier League would find its way back into its own coffers – United's share of TV revenue under the current contract has typically been around seven per cent.

Ultimately the bid was blocked because BSkyB ran out of political capital with the regulatory authorities. Contrary to expectations and some comment at the time, it was not a political decision by a Labour government piqued at the hostile stance taken by Murdoch papers against the euro. Such was the depth and intensity of the MMC's opposition to the deal that backing the commission's recommendation was the easiest decision any DTI minister was ever likely to have to take.

The decision left BSkyB frustrated, Murdoch angered (in a fit of pique he blamed Sam Chisholm, the former BSkyB boss, for upsetting the MMC in previous encounters with the competition authorities) and Manchester United's management bewildered. While the anti-bid campaigners rejoiced, the club was left to ponder an uncertain future.

Alex Ferguson's team soon came to the management's rescue, its remarkable exploits at home and in Europe pushing concerns about the club's future to the back of most people's minds. The Old Trafford bosses also moved quickly to reassert their commercial independence, unveiling a series of licensing, merchandising and retail deals in east

Asia and the middle east as part of an ambitious programme to spread the Red Devils brand far and wide.

However, a nagging worry remained. In stock market parlance, the club was still very much "in play". Martin Edwards, United's chief executive and largest single shareholder, had agreed to sell his 14 per cent stake to BSkyB. That sale was scuppered by the MMC, but to financiers, ambitious investment bankers and anyone with a spare billion dollars to hand, Edwards was still a seller looking for a buyer. That meant United was still ripe for takeover.

Against such a background, those who manned the barricades against Murdoch remained vigilant. Calls for Edwards to sell his shares to fans or place them in a trust to safeguard the club against another takeover bid went unheeded, while heavy hitters from the business world started taking a renewed interest in United shares, like big cats circling a wounded prey. Virtually unassailable on the field, England's biggest club remained dangerously vulnerable off it.

little decisions
piers pennington

Down at the grass roots, the local council proved a trickier opponent even than 13-year-old Paul Ince wannabes

June 1998
Picture a scene of total chaos as 200 footballers swarm around a few harassed looking organisers seeking advice and guidance. Some of the players show signs of skill, but many appear never to have kicked a ball before. It could be a Manchester City training session from any time in the past three years, except that the players are all under the age of 13 and the grown-ups can still raise a smile from time to time.

It is, in fact, the Kingston Little League trials for 1998-99; football at the grassroots and the lifeblood of the game, as it occasionally suits the FA to claim. The League's managers are out in force to spot talent, but the biting wind and persistent drizzle are obscuring the players' numbers, with the result that any nine-year old capable of beating a couple of opponents is pursued down the touch-line by scary-looking men and women (well, one woman – but still scary) yelling "Name!" and scribbling on note-pads.

The council has contributed to the fun by failing to mow the pitch, so that the smaller players can only be identified by hair colour. When the grass is finally cut a few days later, three seven-year-olds are found still trying to perfect that Cruyff turn which will get them a place in the Intermediate Hoops. Specialist goalkeepers, or at least anybody that is prepared to play in goal, are particularly in demand and it is rumoured that one particularly unscrupulous manager, spotting an unsuspecting lad in a David Seaman top on his way to the trials, has bundled him into an unmarked white van and driven him home to secure his signature.

Eventually darkness falls, the players drift home dreaming of glory and the managers skulk away for the mysterious ritual known as The Pick, an exercise which involves strong drink, stronger language and a suspiciously battered pack of playing cards to decide who gets first choice.

September
The big kick-off. It used to be simple – a six-team league, three games on a Saturday morning, 25 minutes each way, start at 9.30, finish by 12.30, time for a drink and go to a match in the afternoon. Now, in addition to the main league, there are 12 Intermediate teams, six seven-a-side teams (in preparation for 1999-2000, when under-tens are not allowed to play 11-a-side) and a Bantams section offering training and practice matches for the younger children. Start at 9.00, finish by 2.30 if you're lucky and no chance of getting to any ground except Kingstonian.

Foolishly agree to referee the first match and you are likely to be stuck on the pitch for five hours. The League's roster of players has grown from 84 children to more than 450 and still we have a waiting list. This suggests that enthusiasm for the game is as strong as ever but that schools, particularly primary schools, no longer have the time, the facilities or the inclination to meet the demand for organised football.

October

The rumours which have been circulating for months prove to be true – there is a proposal to build a school on the field used by our Bantams section. At the council's Education and Leisure committee, the school's governors paint a picture of Dickensian conditions in their present premises: leaky roofs; outside toilets; pinched, shivering, little faces, fingers too frozen to drag the chalk over the slate. We counter with images of these same children on a Saturday morning at Bantams, the only enjoyment they have in life – how can the council take it away from them? After several hours two of the three political parties come up with an alternative plan and the field is saved.

Meanwhile, in the outside world it has rained for several weeks and the pitches are often unplayable. On one of the rare days we are able to start the matches one manager concedes the game before half-time, having noticed that his team, cold and drenched, are no longer playing but are just standing there crying, something you rarely see in the Premiership (Nottingham Forest against Manchester United being an obvious exception).

December 1998/January 1999

There is a dramatic end to the first half of the season (a new league competition begins in January) as four of the six teams in the main league finish level on points, causing a frantic checking and rechecking of results to confirm the rankings on goal difference. In one of the vital last matches, a lippy 13-year-old ponders rather too loudly on the prospects of having a referee who isn't on drugs and is sent off. This means an automatic three-match suspension, but the referee's report recommends clemency, as dissent would normally merit only a yellow card.

A one-match suspension is agreed, but not all the teams' managers get to hear about it, with the result that in January the player in question pops in five goals against a team that hadn't expected him to be on the pitch. All hell is let loose at the next League meeting, with threats of resignation and referral to the FA, UEFA, the Pope and Andy Gray. After several hours and pints it is decided that the player concerned will miss the return match later in the season; it's the best argument we've had in a long time, and we all vow to do it more often in the future.

March

Wimbledon have sent us complimentary tickets for their league match against Leicester and around 200 Bantams and seven-a-siders, accompanied by parents and managers, make the trek across to Selhurst Park. For many (including some parents) it is their first taste of the Premiership, and when Steve Guppy rifles the ball into the top corner from 25 yards after ten minutes we all settle down to enjoy the feast of skilful and exciting football which only these highly-paid professionals can provide.

Sadly, the only lessons our youngsters are able to take away from the afternoon are that when you are 1-0 up away from home, your sole ambition is to stop the opposition playing; and that in these circumstances it is more helpful to be the size of Ian Marshall rather than Michael Hughes, something their own experiences have already led them to suspect.

We now hear that central government, supposedly committed to preserving playing fields at all costs, have rejected the council's compromise solution to the provision of extra classroom space, have instructed them to look again at the proposal to build a school on our field and, most alarmingly of all, have hinted at the likelihood of funds being made available for the building.

So it's back to the grindstone of petitions, letter writing, public meetings and planning procedures. All this and a backlog of fixtures to catch up on by Easter, which means playing on Sundays and weekday evenings as well as Saturdays. At least Alex Ferguson gets paid to moan about it.

May

Three excellent weekends in a row to finish the season on a high note. On May 2nd we are at Kingstonian, who have not only sponsored us but made available their ground for our cup finals. The weather is fine, the players (and referees) experience the thrill of having real dressing rooms and a tunnel from which to emerge on to the pitch and the parents are kept safely in the stands instead of in their usual position about five yards inside the touchline. The games are hard fought and exciting and the bar staff are stunned by the demands made on them by the Little League committee.

The following week we hold a six-a-side tournament on the threatened field, with four pitches symbolically marked out on the site of the proposed school. Unfortunately, the plans prove to have been revised, and the school is now scheduled to be built on the area occupied by the beer tent, the barbecue and the bouncy castle. Nonetheless it is an impressive display of what will be lost if the field is sacrificed, with hundreds of children playing more than 70 matches and generally having a good time. Again the weather is fine, all the food and drink runs out and several councillors are there to have their ears bent before the meeting to decide the future of the field in June.

Then on May 15th it's off to Wembley for Kingstonian's big day. Little League fill a couple of coaches for the FA Trophy final, which Kingstonian duly win, albeit somewhat luckily. The real highlight of the day is the warm-up match: Black Bull Taverners against the ironically named Swansea Boys Club in the final of the veterans competition. To the kids it's just a load of fat, bald, old men struggling to run the length of the pitch, but for the rest of us it's the only chance we'll ever have to witness on the sacred turf players with whom we can truly identify.

Next week Manchester United will be starring here in the second leg of the most over-hyped footballing achievement of the century, but today it's a good day out for people who still believe in playing football for pleasure. Some Little Leaguers may follow in the footsteps of Steven Reid, now playing in the Second Division with Millwall. But if others still feel the urge in 40 years time to keep those creaking knees going because they can't bear to stop playing the game they love, then our modest efforts will not have been in vain.

suddenly,
no one likes us
neil hurden

Fulham fans had to pay the price of success. In their case, losing the patronising affection of most of the rest of the league

Pre-match or half-time entertainment is an acquired taste at the best of times. Before the game you want to concentrate in peace on cultivating that vaguely reassuring sense of anxiety which is the vital emotional accompaniment to all but the most routine of games. While at half-time, the manager's programme notes are always there jumping out to challenge the intellect.

I am generally happy to tolerate the penalty competitions between tiny children which have become a ritual at Craven Cottage. If nothing else, it gives the impressively effervescent David Hamilton something to organise. However, if things get any more ambitious, deeply reactionary thoughts tend to spring to the fore.

There was a time, not so long ago, during what some historians are already calling our "Dark Ages", when the balance between marketing and traditional standards of entertainment slipped so far out of kilter that a Craven Cottage crowd was introduced to Su Pollard and Gareth

Hunt in some crazed and irresponsible experiment with our emotions. They may even have been there on the same occasion, and there was probably a Gladiator or two involved too, although you can never be quite sure when reliving memories that deeply repressed.

All of which brings me to the one event last season which seems to have captured the interest of the non-Fulham supporting classes even more than the club's century of league points or the eternal debate over Little Kev's career plans. As everyone knows, the home game against Wigan saw a slightly bemused Michael Jackson treading the very same turf as Su and Gareth, hiding his modesty and sheltering from the intense early April sun beneath an improbably large black and white umbrella, lent to him by a friendly but persistent Egyptian shop owner.

When you are looking for symbolism to illustrate the recent change in fortunes of Fulham FC, it doesn't come much more blatant than this. There has been an almost stratospheric leap up the ladder of success and publicity, but one which has occasionally left a vaguely disconcerting aftertaste.

Last season presented two major challenges to the Fulham supporter. First, it was a challenge as much as anything else to our own sense of credulity. Fulham fans are not temperamentally well attuned to seeing their team win 14 home games on the trot or amass 101 points, let alone watching their manager being pursued by chequebook-waving officials from an increasingly desperate FA.

Historically, if the club has done well, the accepted style has been to scrape promotion by the narrowest of margins, as in 1982, or at the very least conspire to lose out on the championship at the last hurdle, as in 1997 or 1971. Of course, we have generally been more adept at missing out altogether, as we did in the season before last and, most distressingly of all, in falling one point short of promotion to the old First Division in 1983. There are even some fans who would argue, a little too dogmatically perhaps, that that was why they chose the club in the first place.

The other major affront to our traditional self-image has been the complete reversal in other fans' attitudes to Fulham. As it would probably be phrased at the New Den: "No one likes us (any more); We do care."

Although a fairly healthy spirit of disregard developed during the Dark Ages from the general direction of Brentford, it is fair to say that a lot of other supporters seemed to retain a soft spot for the club, no doubt a mixture of admiration for our fine sportsmanlike traditions and the enduring appeal of a home banker.

Consequently, being viewed as the moral equivalent of the Man Utd of the Second Division has been a chastening experience. This season's mantra from away fans, the witty "Where were you when you were shit ?" plagued us throughout. In fact it took until the final game of the season for the challenge to be taken up, thanks to Kevin Moore, our former centre-back and now training ground manager (well, it beats running a pub). Tongue firmly in cheek, he strode on to the pitch at half-time, pushing several small penalty-taking children aside, and politely asked the hordes from Preston to desist from The Chant, as it was particularly upsetting for those like him who had actually been on the pitch "when we were shit".

Perhaps even more dispiriting, though, than the away fans' dirge was the usual variant on the theme of *Blue Moon* from some in the Hammersmith End, a little something along the lines of "You'll never play here again". In some ways this can be explained as a self-defence mechanism. It does, however, suggest a worryingly complacent grasp of the concept of nemesis. It is also almost too painfully (and usually unintentionally) ironic for comfort, given the fact that it was only a few years ago that it was we who faced the prospect of never playing at the Cottage again.

Perhaps it was the difficulties in adjusting to our new status which meant that in many ways the Cup adventures were more uplifting than the league campaign. It seems vaguely, if not completely, ungrateful, after waiting so long for a season of such domination, to qualify this success in any way. However, after the initial excitement of realising that this was going to be a special season, following victories over Man

City and early leaders Stoke, there was a sense of relentless progression rather than inspiration about the home league campaign in particular.

Although the team did put together spells of exciting football, much of the success was built on an efficient and dominating central defence of Chris Coleman, Simon Morgan and Kit Symons, with Maik Taylor developing, as a new Northern Ireland international, a nice line in stereotypical Ulster stubbornness in goal. The Keegan myth, of creating teams enthused with a gung-ho spirit of attack but with defences ever ready to add to the general amusement of the wider public, could not have been better dispelled.

In many ways, of course, it was a huge pleasure to see a highly dominant defensive machine in action, once you had got over the surreal notion that they were playing in white shirts. It's all very well being vaguely appreciated by others, but when you have witnessed cult figures (and I think we all know what that means) like Jim Hicks and Sean Gore in what could loosely be described as "action", you take a certain pride in seeing someone of the stature of Coleman at the heart of your defence.

Nevertheless, real excitement did not emerge, for me at least, until the FA Cup campaign took off. Again, past experiences suggested disappointment was about to jump up and cuff us firmly but fairly around the head. Ever since the Cup final in 1975, our only brief flirtation with Cup success came in a closely contested fourth round tie against Watford in 1983. Having narrowly missed out on a fifth round place, thanks to Dean Coney's more than adequate impression of Norman Wisdom in front of a gaping Watford goal, we finally fell to a rather beautiful winner in the replay from John Barnes, in those heady days when he followed the radical approach of running forwards with the ball. More recently, headlines have been made only by the Hayes and Yeovil "incidents".

Although a first round draw against Leigh RMI did not bode particularly well, this game set the tone for the rest of the Cup run. Strangely, the inspiration came from a member of the opposing team in the improbably large shape of their veteran goalkeeper, David Felgate, who pulled off a succession of such unbelievable saves that you had no choice but to give up banging your head in frustration against the terrace crush barriers and just relax and enjoy the display. Quite why Peter Schmeichel has attracted such attention when there is someone much better and even larger only a few miles away in the Northern Premier defeats me.

Fortunately, the magical spirit which had taken residence in the gloves of the Great Felgate was partly exorcised and we triumphed in the replay before the refreshing unpredictability of the Cup took hold again with a narrow victory against Hartlepool. The thrill of beating Southampton in the third round was somewhat diluted by the fact that we had already added to their early season nightmares by dispatching them from the League Cup, and so we still travelled to Villa Park for the fourth round in a blissful state of naivety, having stocked up in advance on every available justification for failure against the recently stalled Premiership pace-setters.

This turned out to be the defining moment of the season, however, when sheer excitement took over from the satisfying but steady feeling of near invincibility which characterised the latter part of the league campaign. After several minutes of trying to refocus on the sight of our team playing in a stadium which appeared vertical rather than horizontal in design, a wonderful thing happened, which caused a very little and very eccentric woman standing on her seat next to me, whom I had never met before in my life, to embrace me like a mother greeting her son's return from the Western Front.

Appropriately for a great Fulham occasion the inspiration was Simon Morgan, our longest-serving player and, although not our most skilful and far from our most expensive, the man with the link to our pre-Fayed past. The perfection of the moment was heightened by the fact that I was sitting in a line directly behind the trajectory of the header which skimmed off our hero's head and sped through the small gap between the top of the straining head of the Villa defender guarding the right hand post and the bottom of the crossbar. If it were possible, things got even better from then on with a Steve Hayward free-kick and a second half display of competitiveness and control which transported the away end to a distant and blissful place.

On the coach home I sat next to a young bloke who seemed even more stunned by the whole occasion than I was. Approximately every ten miles or so, one of us would turn to the other and say "I just don't believe that really happened", then shake our head slowly and settle back into silence. We took this in turn on a strict rota basis and managed gradually to reduce the frequency to once every 20 minutes or so by the time we neared London. It took a while to break the habit completely, though, and if you happen to travel to work on the Northern Line, there is a fair chance I may have mentioned something along the same lines to you the following week.

By contrast the Theatre of Dreams experience in the fifth round a few weeks later was interesting but somehow less invigorating, and not just because we lost narrowly. Keegan had already started his slow and slippery politician's exit from the club and we were missing a number of our best players. Nevertheless, had John Salako, one of our less successful big name buys, been able to hit his ten-yard drive just a few more inches above the surface, we may possibly all have been spared one of the three legs of the Treble.

Far more of you might still have liked us then.

role your own

joyce woolridge

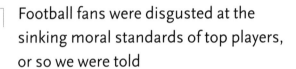

Football fans were disgusted at the
sinking moral standards of top players,
or so we were told

The allegations I am about to make concern top-class,
famous internationals, highly respected throughout
the world. They involve drug-taking and alcohol.
Furthermore, I am prepared to name names, so convinced am I of the
impeccable credentials of my sources.

Before an important FA Cup tie the leading player of a midlands
team is stricken by a particularly severe bout of flu. He goes to the
manager and tells him there is no chance of him playing; his legs are
weak and he won't be able to last the 90 minutes. The manager sends
for a medical specialist, so much is riding on the game.

The doctor takes the player to one side. He gives him two capsules
which he describes as "pep pills" of a type sometimes given to air force
pilots on long range missions. The winger takes the tablets as instructed
one hour before the game and is able to play for the entire match
without ill effects, though the "medication" is so strong he is unable
to sleep and paces his room frenetically throughout the night.

A centre forward for a top northern club regularly drinks alcohol in the dressing room a few minutes before the kick-off in full view of his team-mates. During the World Cup he knows that the FIFA drug tests will show up the substance in his urine. Unable to do without his usual pre-match lift, he prevails on one of his fellow players to break open an ammonia capsule for him which he sniffs deeply to give him the desired buzz.

Usually articles which begin like this would coyly leave the reader to guess the identity of these two prominent players. I am not prepared to adopt the usual cop-out. The "midlands winger" is none other than the wizard of the dribble, that model of asceticism and knight of football, Sir Stanley Matthews, a man whose dedication and morality have been continually held up as a shining example of how professionals should conduct themselves.

The year was 1946 and Stoke City were seriously worried by the prospect of facing Sheffield United without their superstar and talisman. The Luftwaffe had apparently ingested the medicine which allowed Stan to keep up his mazy dribbles before their bombing missions on Britain. This revelation was not unearthed from any obscure, previously suppressed source; Matthews cheerfully described his pill-popping and its curious after-effects in *Feet First*, his "long-awaited" autobiography, published in 1948.

One of British football's other knights and now its most respected world ambassador, Sir Bobby Charlton, chronicled his pre-match tippling in *Forward For England*, a post-1966 cash-in. A glass of sherry five minutes before running out eased his throat, he tells us, and made it easier for him to breathe at the start of play. George Best, in the cheesily titled *The Good, the Bad and the Bubbly* says Bobby also drank a couple of shots of whisky, though presumably not on top of the sherry. Best was not trying to shock readers, but simply describing how players dealt with pre-match nerves – Nobby Stiles took out his false teeth, Brian Kidd threw up and Sir Bobby reached for the bottle.

Charlton also admits to ten cigarettes a day, an indulgence which he recognises could be bad for him, but does not affect his wind because he is so fit. Ray Wilson and Charlton enacted a solemn ritual in which Ray threw Bobby's boots to him one by one and then proffered the stimulant. Because of superstition they continued it throughout England's World Cup-winning campaign. Contrast the indifference which greeted these autobiographical confessions of what made Bobby and Stanley run with the hysteria which accompanies similar, though often lesser, transgressions today.

Contemporary media coverage of each football season appears to fall into categories. We survived "the season of sleaze" in 1994-95, when critics of all kinds agonised as their nostrils were filled with the sour stench of corruption from the stadia and boardrooms of England. Last season was the season of moral outrage when everyone, it seems, was "disgusted" by the behaviour of professionals.

It began with denunciations of Paul Gascoigne's kebab and lager pre-World Cup benders, accompanied by his "loathsome lieutenants" Chris Evans and Danny Baker. Debates raged about whether a kebab and pitta bread packed with salad was a suitable snack for a player whose fitness was soon to be put to the ultimate test against the cream of world football's athletes. Nutritionists who annoyingly said that it wasn't that bad were ignored. The final nail in his international coffin was hammered in when he admitted that he smoked.

Soon afterwards, bleached-out, fuzzy photos of Teddy Sheringham holidaying privately on the Algarve adorned some front pages, leaving the deeply shocked British public in no doubt that here was another squad member whose body was not his temple. Gascoigne's "bloated" condition was denounced from the tabloid pulpits; Sheringham's spare frame, without a discernible millimetre of fat, gave them a few more problems, so the vague effects of late nights and sexual activity on stamina and wind were lamented.

Since then we have also been "totally disgusted" by Stan Collymore's depression, which his allies had to start prefacing with the phrase "clinical" to counter the widespread view that depression is a synonym for petulance or "not knowing how lucky you are". How strange it is that no religious guru has formulated ten commandments for perfect happiness which include "Thou shalt be on 20 grand a week" and "Thou shalt wear Armani" as, according to popular opinion, this is all you need for bliss.

On the subject of theology, "Hoddle's twaddle" about reincarnation "completely disgusted" us all. It was, of course, a piece of arrant nonsense he cooked up with his spiritual advisor (who must be a charlatan as she is a middle aged woman called Eileen) and not a religious belief shared by millions for centuries. Liverpool and West Ham players at private Christmas parties were also paraded for our distaste, full of shocking images such as Paul Ince being a restraining influence and Neil Ruddock in a gold lamé jumpsuit.

Finally, in April, Robbie Fowler ensured that the season of disgust ended with outrage levels at the maximum. This was not engendered chiefly by his homophobic remarks and actions. Instead, it was simulation of certain activities, rather than the activities themselves, which resulted in a suspension and loud condemnation.

Past goal celebrations have involved simulating dogs urinating on the pitch, smoking a "celebratory cigar" (though it is generally accepted that Gordon Strachan was actually simulating the action of telling the Kop to fuck off), downing pints of lager, diving, being ducklings and pretending to be a rock and roll star using the corner flag as an imaginary microphone. None of these earned a ban, though many fans prayed devoutly for a life one for Lee Sharpe's Elvis performance. Meanwhile thousands of fans in the crowd are busy simulating masturbation in the general direction of opposing players and match officials without fear of arrest.

You didn't have to be Freud to work out that Fowler's action was a response to the widespread stories about his supposed drug use which he vehemently denies. It was equally obvious that his actions were not going to encourage drug use among the young, nor an outbreak of whitewash snorting on the school playing fields of Merseyside.

The behaviour of Sirs Stanley and Bobby up to 50 years ago would now be pilloried as unacceptable behaviour which would result in action by the authorities. They demonstrate that the widespread belief that such things are "diseases of the modern game" is nonsense. Trevor Ford, the "combative" Welsh centre forward whose speciality was the shoulder charge on goalkeepers, published his equally outspoken views on the Fifties game in the appropriately named *I Lead the Attack* (1957). In the section denouncing the poor training methods of the British coaches, which basically involved tedious lapping, he incidentally revealed that drugs were frequently given to players.

"Some clubs revitalise their players with pep drugs. They've tried oxygen, pheno-barbitone and dexedrine," he asserts. "It's funny how some clubs condone the use of dope and yet the majority frown on the player who smokes or drinks." The equivalent contemporary hypocrisy would, I suppose, be the club which throws out a player who tests positive for cannabis while their doctors continue to pump players full of cortisone.

Hypocrisy isn't the copyright of those running football. I'm loath to believe that the callers to phone-ins, letter writers to newspapers and others who find some vehicle to speak for "ordinary fans" on the television or radio can really be representative of national opinion. Is any adult genuinely "disgusted" by the thought that some footballers smoke fags, drink alcohol, feel stress, have a joint or have sex with consenting adults, even if you don't think some of these activities are a particularly good idea in the few days before an important game?

It seems that not only does football serve as a focus for nationalism and regional identity but, this season, it was increasingly the arena in which standards of behaviour and morality were hammered out. Perhaps the predicted Blairite new puritanism won't be symbolised by an improvement in the probity of politicians or any similarly peripheral figures. Frighteningly, it seems the standard will be set instead by a group of males aged 17 to 30-odd, whose qualification as role models is that they can kick a ball around.

one f in yokohama

justin mccurry

Just as the J-League was gaining credibility on the field, the club owners began to lose their nerve. It was time for the fans to take things into their own hands

In sport, as much as in politics, success on the international stage is no guarantor of domestic bliss, as recent events in Japan demonstrate. In the same month that Japan finished heroic runners-up in the World Youth Championship in Nigeria and Jubilo Iwata lifted the Asian Club Championship in Iran, the J-League was approaching the season's midway point at the most precarious juncture in its seven-year existence.

At the peak of Japan's economic boom ten years ago, when Tokyo real estate prices read like telephone numbers and baseball was the armchair sport of choice, any talk of "professional football" and "recession" would have required a considerable leap of imagination. Not any more. Although Japan's sporting *lingua franca* still reverberates with speculation about pennant races and fresh-faced pitching prodigies, on the economic front, the self-confidence of the bubble era has been replaced by such nasty, alien words as "unemployment" and "restructuring". All of which, at least for the country's football lovers, has created an untimely and very real sense of anxiety over the fate of Japan's experiment with the game as it prepares, with South Korea, to greet the rest of the world's football community in 2002.

Predictions by cynics that the professional game in Japan would be nothing more than a faddish flirtation for fans and a money-making exercise for the corporate world appeared to be borne out at the start of the 1999 season when the Japan Football Association released a depressing litany of statistics. Merchandise sales had slumped from 3.6 billion yen (£18 million) in 1993, to just 324 million yen (£1.6 million) in 1998. Gate receipts, too, had fallen drastically as crowds declined from an average of 19,598 in 1994 to 11,982 in 1998.

That all was not well had been made clear at the end of the previous season, when the *Yomiuri* newspaper announced it was to sell its 49 per cent stake in Kawasaki Verdy, who had accumulated debts of more than two billion yen. Verdy, it should be remembered, were not small-timers. They are one of Japan's best known and most successful teams, having won five amateur titles as Yomiuri FC and the J-League in 1993 and 1994. They spawned several of the national side's best players, notably Kazuyoshi "Kazu" Miura, later of Croatia Zagreb.

Verdy, though, had a disastrous end to the 1998 season, finishing second to bottom with only nine points from a possible 51, prefacing the split with the *Yomiuri*. Predictably, the team's squad began to disintegrate once it became clear that the astronomical salaries some players had been earning were no longer available. By the start of the 1999 season, the playing staff had been reduced from 40 to 31, including eight teenagers.

Verdy proceeded to breathe new life into the increasingly untenable adage, in football at least, that money cannot always buy success. Under South Korean coach Kunihide Lee, they confounded pundits, and probably surprised themselves, by topping the table at the beginning of May, followed by perennial championship prospects Jubilo Iwata.

Although Verdy survived and prospered from their rude awakening, the same cannot be said for fellow J-League founders Yokohama Flugels. One of the Flugels' co-sponsors, yet another construction firm, decided to withdraw financial backing at the end of the 1998 season, blaming the economic slump and poor attendances. The Flugels did not disappear altogether, although, in the eyes of many of their fans, their eventual fate was no more palatable. The club's officials, as if speaking of two financially troubled subcontractors, announced that the former Asia Super Cup winners would be merged with local rivals Yokohama Marinos. The Flugels' main sponsor, All Nippon Airways (ANA), would take a 30 per cent share in the new club, with 70 per cent going to Marinos' longtime backers Nissan.

By the start of the 1999 season, the Flugels' presence had been reduced to a mere "F" in the name of the new club, Yokohama F Marinos. Imagine Manchester City being swallowed up by their wealthier, more successful neighbours to become Manchester C United, and you begin to get an idea of the magnitude of the fans' distress. The fans themselves earned widespread praise, not least from JFA President Shunichiro Okano, for their commendable but ultimately ineffectual attempts to save their team from the merger.

Fans were particularly angered by the hasty and autocratic manner in which the merger was decided – most learned of their team's fate in the newspapers. And so, in what should have been a perfect start to New Year celebrations – a victory in the Emperor's Cup final on January 1st – Flugels fans watched their team lift the trophy knowing they had probably seen captain Motohiro Yamaguchi and his men take to the pitch together for the last time.

Shimizu S-Pulse and their manager Steve Perryman made admirable attempts to make a game of the final, aware that anything other than a defeat for them would not just be unfortunate, but grossly unjust in the eyes of a sentimental viewing public. The fact that towards the end of the 1998 season Flugels were beginning to play the kind of mature football the J-League had been striving for during its first six seasons added to the growing sense of exasperation with the behaviour of the club's administrators and sponsors. With eight consecutive league and cup wins under their belts in the run-up to the Emperor's Cup final, this was without a doubt a team about to be cut down in its prime.

Even Flugels' German manager Gert Engels felt the need to breach his strictly coaching brief and comment. After his team's last home game, a 2-1 win over Avispa Fukuoka at Mitsuzawa Stadium, Engels told the 13,000 home crowd: "I wish next season we can meet again. If we don't, our victory in the Emperor's Cup, Asian Cup-Winners Cup and Asian Super Cup will be lost," before urging ANA and the league to do "everything possible" to save the club.

The players, not known for a willingness to discuss matters off the pitch, indulged in what was threatening to descend into a frenzy of biting the corporate hands that would no longer feed them. In an emotional plea many Japanese would have struggled to sympathise with before the rot of recession started eating into the country's lifetime employment system, one player told the crowd: "I have a two-year-old daughter and a family to support, and I am boiling over with anger because all the players feel ignored and cheated by the owners."

His sense of outrage was shared by most, if not all, the fans present. One told reporters: "I love the Flugels and the Marinos, so next season will not be a problem for me." Fans less given to such contrariness had already collected more than 40,000 signatures supporting the "Save The Flugels" campaign. Predictably, their plea fell on deaf ears and, by the end of the same day, all hopes of a last-minute reprieve vanished when the club announced the merger documents had been signed.

Only seven Flugels made the transition to F Marinos for the 1999 season. It is more difficult to say how many of the team's fans were persuaded to make a clean break and back the new team, who were soon being tipped as title contenders. In any case, it soon became clear that a hardcore following of around 1,500 had other plans that would spare like-minded fans unwanted soul-searching. The fans, backed by sympathetic players and officials and led by a bookish freelance scriptwriter, applied to the JFA to form a new team, Yokohama FC, who deserve additional credit for being one of the very few Japanese teams to avoid an ill-advised embellishment of their name.

With no prospective sponsors in sight, they decided to pool resources and lay the club's financial foundations themselves. By the time the Flugels performed their swansong in the Emperor's Cup final, the fledgling club's volunteer backroom staff of company employees, housewives and students had collected half a million signatures of support and about 67 million yen in donations. Aware that public sympathy would only take them so far, the club turned to US sports manangement firm IMG for help. They later secured the the appointment of former German international Pierre Littbarski as manager.

Yokohama's admission into the JFL in February was completed with almost unseemly haste, although it had fulfilled certain requirements, such as arranging a minimum number of home fixtures, finding no fewer than five "home" grounds and putting together a squad of 23 youngsters and cast-offs from struggling J-League clubs.

The circumstances of the club's formation, and the appointment of Littbarski, ensured unprecedented media interest for a club playing in the country's unofficial Third Division. Littbarski was well suited to the task of rekindling past glories. In the mid-1990s, during the J-League's boom years, he was one of the game's highest-profile foreign imports, even gracing the nation's television screens in advertisements for German sausages. After going into coaching he became one of the few foreign sports stars in Japan to take the trouble of learning the language.

To augment the donations made by fans, Yokohama negotiated sponsorship deals with Citibank and the car parts manufacturer, Bosch. It also pulled off a minor coup by securing coverage of some of its league matches on satellite television. On the pitch, the club's quest to regain J-League status began reasonably well, with a 2-2 draw against Jatco FC in front of a home crowd of more than 11,000, followed by an away win against the improbably named Hollyhock Mito.

The irony of the Flugels' demise is that the financial rug has been swept from beneath the feet of Japanese professional football just at the time when the standard of play had finally begun to earn plaudits from abroad and the players themselves were attracting the interest of European clubs. Yet another round of expansion had brought a certain authenticity and competitiveness to a league that began with just ten clubs, untroubled by the possibility of messy relegation fights or tiresome draws. Now, two teams are to be relegated from the 16-strong J1 to the ten-team J2, from which two in turn will gain automatic promotion.

JFA President Okano called on players, administrators and fans to make 1999 Japanese football's "renaissance year". Jubilo and the nation's youth team have already responded in kind, but what of the J-League? The country's economic mess and the changes it heralded certainly hurt, but the signs are that they are also beginning to work. Even foreign managers, often sceptical of Japan's willingness to adapt, appear to believe that the game's crisis is now one of confidence as much as economics.

Hiroshima Sanfrecce's manager Eddie Thomson (formerly coach of the Australian national team) has little sympathy for what he sees as the self-inflicted predicament of Yokohama FC et al, but is confident of a recovery in fan and media interest once they realise the homegrown players are capable of producing the kind of football once considered the preserve of Zico, Lineker, Dunga and Littbarski. Now, when foreign observers talk of improvements in the skill and strength of Japanese players, most do so without implying that, well, they couldn't really get much worse.

The Olympic qualifiers and, of course, the World Cup, will ensure football remains a financial risk worth taking in the short-term. But if there is a lesson to be learned from the Flugels debacle, it is that authorities will have to start addressing the needs of fans if popular interest in the game is to be sustained beyond 2002. For their part, fans must appreciate that, with rights, come the inevitable responsibilities. Japan's Ultra Nippon were among the best organised and best-behaved of all fans at France 98 and, as club supporters, can be relied upon to transform pedestrian suburban stadiums throughout Japan into cauldrons of colour and sound.

The 51,000 who turned out to watch the Jubilo v Antlers game in Tokyo on May 5th are proof enough of that. The fans have the organisational abilities to make their presence felt in new arenas – like television studios and committee rooms – where their interests can be represented and acted on. There could be no better tribute to Flugels fans if Japanese football annals record that the J-League's renaissance, on and off the pitch, began on the despondent terraces of Mitsuzawa Stadium one afternoon at the end of 1998.

the vetch is history
huw richards

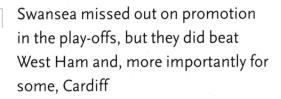

Swansea missed out on promotion
in the play-offs, but they did beat
West Ham and, more importantly for
some, Cardiff

The referees you remember are the ones who do you down. So the name firmly imprinted on every Swansea supporter's mind is Mr Heilbron of Newton Aycliffe, whose handling of a 120th-minute free-kick contributed so signally to Northampton Town's play-off victory a couple of years back. Mr H is doubtless a model citizen who is good to his mother, gives freely to charity and is always ready to lead David Elleray across the road, but his Vetch Field lifetime hostility guarantee is unlikely to expire if and when the Swans move to the new Morfa Stadium.

Perhaps we should also remember those who do us totally undeserved favours. Let's hear it then for Mr Taylor of Cheshunt, the 1998-99 arbiter of the Welsh version of Walpurgis morning otherwise known as Swansea City v Cardiff City. Perhaps we would still have had a cup run, and Cyril the Swan would have become famous, even if Mr Taylor had sent off Matthew Bound. But it seems unlikely.

Bound should certainly have gone for taking out John Williams when he was the last man in defence. Anyone familiar with the flying postman knew a goal was far from certain, but a clear chance was unquestionably denied. Quite why Mr Taylor did not issue a red is a mystery, but Bound stayed on and the Swans, lucky to be only one down when five would have been a fairer reflection of the first half, came back to win with a late goal from... Matthew Bound.

In the long run it didn't matter to Cardiff. They went up anyway and, annoyingly enough, they deserved it. There is little doubt the three automatic promotion places went to the three best sides in the Third. But it mattered immensely to Swansea. Far too much weight is placed upon matches against Cardiff. Taking four points off them was great fun, but they got the prize that really mattered.

The only thing more tedious than the return match at Cardiff was the witless name-calling, seen at its most pathetic in the letters column of *Wales on Sunday*, between the braindead and the one-eyed on both sides. But there is still a peculiar pleasure in doing them when you don't deserve it – a point missed by the metropolitan prat from the *Telegraph* in a report of monumental, condescending silliness.

Losing to Cardiff would have kept the Swans pinned in lower-mid table – an uncomfortable location in a season with no catastrophically bad team around to relax the rest of the strugglers. The Cup run had already begun with a 3-0 win over Millwall, but the real momentum came with the win against Cardiff in November and lasted, with the odd springtime hiccup, until extra-time at Glanford Park in the play-offs six months later.

It was also a crucial step towards the acceptance of John Hollins by the fans. It had been a relief when Alan Cork was fired after two-thirds of a season of tactical incoherence, and then – as an occasional QPR-watcher – when reports that Ray Wilkins was the designated successor proved false. But initial results under Hollins had been moderate and he had been outmanoeuvred in the first half of the derby by Cardiff manager Frank Burrows – still warmly remembered at the Vetch whatever the legally unprintable song sung by the North Bank choir might imply.

Hollins's ability to adjust, and his evident joy at the result, won him a lot of respect and affection and helped start to exorcise the outsized ghost of Jan Molby. Hollins's desire to identify fully with his club and its supporters was underlined later in the same week at the launch of a biography of Ivor Allchurch, the greatest of all Swans heroes. Hollins not only turned up but stayed far longer than convention demanded and chatted happily to anyone.

Hollins got much better results from a squad which looked so bedraggled under Cork. He was lucky that the best things Cork did were to complete his last two signings – centre-half Jason Smith from Tiverton and midfielder Martin Thomas from Fulham. But he also transformed part of his inheritance. Steve Watkin, previously much more immovable object than irresistible force, began to look like the intelligent, ball-holding striker who scored the winner for Wrexham against Arsenal in 1992. Michael Howard, a full-back previously sufficiently anonymous that some thought he was also working as shadow foreign secretary, became a solidly consistent element in the best Swans defence in years. Admittedly some players did not improve, although midfielder Jon Coates's confidence could hardly be expected to survive the blow of discovering that Bobby Gould thought he could play.

The Cardiff victory slotted two other pieces into place. It says something about Swansea's attacking weaknesses over the previous season that they had never adequately replaced Steve Torpey, who had taken his arthritic dromedary impersonation off to Bristol City for a laughably large fee in summer 1997. Julian Alsop, signed from Bristol Rovers, had been tried but looked no better than Torpey, which is why he started on the bench against Cardiff. His arrival after half-time helped transform the game.

It wasn't just that he won everything in the air but that, unlike most lower division target men – who even when they win the ball distribute it pretty much at random – he showed the ability to place headers precisely. Just such a header created the equaliser for the second revelation, Martin Thomas. Thomas had so far looked the classic lower division bits and pieces midfielder – hard working and competitive but without ever really convincing that the bits added up to a decent player. For him, too, Cardiff marked the transformation.

At their best Hollins's team developed a measured, controlled pattern of play that served them particularly well against teams from higher divisions. Derby County, in the FA Cup fourth round, were the first higher division team in seven matches in serious competitions (excluding the Auto Windscreens Trophy even if we did win it once) to beat them inside 90 minutes. Cork's team had the sort of disciplinary record you associate with South Central Los Angeles street gangs, or Arsenal. Hollins's also had their moments, but it was a long time before we saw the once-familiar sight of the Swans finishing with ten men.

Big clubs twitch nervously at the phrase "giant killer", while smaller ones rather like it. In this respect Swansea retain big club credentials. Our cup runs have been infrequent, our collection of scalps – West Brom, Crystal Palace, Middlesbrough – hardly the sort that create lifelong memories. On the other side of the ledger is a long roll of dishonour including Nuneaton Borough (twice) and a whole litany of pain at the hands of slightly tatty seaside resorts – Minehead, Margate and even Colwyn Bay, who took John Toshack's Football League leaders to a deeply embarrassing Welsh Cup replay.

There was no great shock about beating Stoke, in steep decline after their strong start, at the Vetch. But the two third round games against West Ham take some believing, even given the Hammers' serial incompetence against the lower orders. Not only were they three divisions higher, but they were placed, and would finish, higher in their division than we did in ours.

You look at a lineup containing Berkovic, Wright, Hartson, Sinclair and wonder how a team round about midway in the Third can possibly cope. The idea that we might get the better of them twice was positively outlandish. So too was the possibility that 3,000 Swans fans might make more noise than roughly seven times that number of East Enders. Tardiness in putting in for tickets might have deprived me of a place among them, but the overflow press box on halfway at least provided the ideal location for ascertaining that they really were making most of the noise. Morriston Orpheus they're not, and the repertoire tends far more to *Falling in Love With You* than *Calon Lan*. However, as at Newcastle four seasons ago, there was still a volume and an approximation to tunefulness that, even more than the quality of the team's performance, made an impression on West Ham fans.

We would have settled happily beforehand for 1-1. Yet it felt far more disappointing than the fourth round defeat against Derby would. We couldn't really complain about the Derby result – they played with far more sense and composure than West Ham and we had rarely looked like scoring. But we had outplayed West Ham at Upton Park, permitted by their extraordinary listlessness to play the game at our own slowish pace, and scarcely threatened even after Jason Smith (whose nearest rival for the header was Julian Alsop, rather than any of the Hammers defence) had put us ahead on the hour.

If they had laid siege to Roger Freestone's goal, beating a tattoo on the goalposts and forcing serial goal-line clearances, Julian Dicks's 87th minute equaliser, an optimistic welly from about 30 yards that skidded under Freestone, might have been tolerable. Instead it promised a reversion to normal form at the Vetch and a quick exit. Oh ye of little faith. Yet despite the satisfaction of victory, the West Ham matches may eventually bulk larger in their memories than ours – marking as they did the first team debut of Joe Cole and the final appearances of Hartson, greeted like a hero by Swans fans who recognise him as a North Bank *habitué*, and Dicks.

Cup runs are terrific fun while they last, a break with routine and a chance to upset established orders, raising two fingers at an overrated Premiership, puffed up on Sky money and the self-serving proposition that football started in 1992. They are like those medieval festivals where the lord and master acted as servant to his serfs for the day.

The trouble is that next day you are back to normal life. The cup run was by some margin the best thing about last season. But elements in that success possibly laid the seeds of eventual narrow failure in the league. Having a dominant target-man is great when your midfield is functioning well and he is receiving decent quality service. When the midfield runs out of ideas – around the fifth minute at times later in the season – it is too easy a get-out to belt the ball hopefully in the general direction of his head.

The cup run also gave rise to Cyrilmania. It was a pleasant surprise that a commercial department previously reckoned to combine the imagination of a New Labour MP with the operational competence of a privatised rail operator came up with an idea which attracted national attention. Cyril the Swan threw himself into his role with insane enthusiasm, creating much speculation about his identity. One theory alleged there were two Cyrils who might be identified by differing character traits either side of half time, and the concept of Cyril the Schizoid Swan had a certain charm.

But the phenomenon got out of hand. A Swansea director's statement that "this thing is bigger than all of us" might be excused on the grounds that anything 9ft 4in tall is. But dressing him in a *Sun*-sponsored shirt for the Derby match was a grotesque lapse of taste and judgment and late in the season it looked as though his pre-match antics were part of a conscious winding-up of the crowd.

This was almost certainly counter-productive. For all the talk of "Fortress Vetch", a consistent inability to win at home destroyed any chance of automatic promotion. This was in part due to the creative inadequacies of the midfield but may also have owed something to crowd tension communicating itself to the players.

There were also signs that the concussive volume of the public address system was destroying brain cells on the North Bank. The suspicion of something nasty, first implanted by the booing of Plymouth Argyle's Ronnie Mauge – indistinguishable from the rest of the bunch who ambushed us 3-2 at the Vetch except for his black skin – was confirmed by the appearance of fascist-saluting pond life at the Scunthorpe play-off. Time for the club to show that the anti-racist advert in front of the North Bank is more than lip service.

Next season could be the last at the Vetch. The old ground is faded, has by general acclaim the worst toilets and just about the worst food in the league and has at times looked decidedly uncared for. But it has never been unloved. Constructed to maximise noise levels, it accommodates not only memories of Swans heroes through Jack Fowler to Trevor Ford, Ivor Allchurch and Toshack's teams, but an incomparable atmosphere when there is the slightest thing to shout about.

The move to the planned all-seater Morfa Stadium, another on-off running theme of the last couple of seasons, makes economic sense. But football clubs work on more than balance sheets and unless the best of the Vetch culture can be transported to the Morfa, the losses may outweigh the gains.

What level of football the Morfa will host is hard to predict. In the end the Swans probably got about what they deserved from the season. For the third time a play-off exit might reasonably be put down to a badly-timed in jury – Steve Watkin following Jason Bowen in 1993 and Steve Jones in 1997 – but teams with sufficient depth to handle a higher division shouldn't be so dependent on individuals. It is hard to feel the sense of injustice which followed the Northampton defeat.

So what next? An ideal, perhaps even a logical world, would see this year's progress followed by an automatic promotion campaign, accompanied by the North Bank adopting "We've got an assembly, you've not" in place of its crasser anti-English chants. But long experience shows that if the Swans go up, they always do it by the scenic route.

Contrary to what journalists and TV analysts who never otherwise notice anything outside the Premiership tell us, there is nothing whatsoever magic about going to Wembley for the play-off final. It is getting promotion that is magic, wherever it happens. And naggingly at the back of the mind is the thought that Hereford and Scarborough doubtless thought they were destined for promotion in the seasons that followed play-off semi-final defeats.

export witness

matt nation

The arrival of the Bundesliga's finest in the Premiership might have tilted the balance of Anglo-German football relations decisively. But it didn't

Despite some drawbacks, such as an above-average number of dogs which spew up on public transport, there are many good reasons to live in Germany. On the odd occasion it's handy to be British into the bargain.

BSE, for example, will always ensure that you are well armed for pre-inebriation small-talk at parties with EDP clerks who normally only want to talk about how fast their processor is. There is also a particular brand of anglophile stranger who, although they normally sport the facial expression of Mount Rushmore in a bit of a grouch, will break into little-boy smiles at the sight of an English person, flash a thumbs-up and wax lyrical about Hale and Pace. Even elderly colleagues sidle up to you, put on a gooey voice and beg recipes for pease pudding. You can't grumble, not really.

Until the topic of conversation reaches football, that is. Although it does not belong to that much-cited and extremely large group of countries whose inhabitants are purportedly so fanatical about football that even the stretcher-bearers stop what they're doing to talk about last week's match, Germany nonetheless maintains a healthy interest in the game. When spouting forth on the subject, the population often undergoes the most astonishing transmogrification: computer nerds become razor-sharp trendscouts, perfect strangers' thumbs disappear into overcoat pockets and decrepit workmates loosen their canine's muzzle.

They stare at each other, stare at you, smirk as though your trousers have just fallen down and then kick up the sort of racket which makes even the most boisterous Hare Krishna parade seem like a Remembrance Sunday service. The majority start up the obligatory "Kick and rush, kick and rush" mantra while the frontman interjects apparently arbitrary names and ideas associated with British football: "Nobby Stiles... kick and rush... Wembley goal... kick and rush... Butcher's bandage... kick and rush... like our Horst Hrubesch... kick and rush." It may be matey banter at the moment, but heaven only knows what will happen the day somebody stumbles across old footage of Tommy Smith in full bloom.

Having had to endure this for the best part of a decade, the initial stages of the 1998-99 season had me smacking my chops in anticipation. For it seemed as though half the Bundesliga had converged on British clubs, all enticed by the lure of the propaganda on which they had been raised.

Of course, there had already been a few isolated emigrants, the most prominent being, naturally, Bert Trautmann and Jürgen Klinsmann. But even they were there for reasons which were not quite kosher. Trautmann was the most famous prisoner-of-war to break his neck and Klinsmann's credibility was called into question long before his *contretemps* with Alan Sugar, with a German newspaper admiring his talent "for being able to maintain the image of an alternative globe-trotter pootling around with nothing but a battered old Beetle and a haversack while, at the same time, stuffing his bank account with stonking great wads of money".

But this time it was different. This time our football appeared to have been recognised for the jewel that it has always been. These weren't small-beer rejects on their way to Man City for half a season, nor were they any-port-in-a-storm whores looking for a chance to earn the down-payment on their post-career mini-market. These were real Germans, august young athletes with World Cups and European Championships to their name and flicky passes and shots from their own half and stomach muscles you could break bottles on, who had deigned to come across the North Sea to better themselves and to hell with the wages, however enticingly inflated they may or may not have been.

For a while at least, the bug seemed to have caught on. *Sport-Bild*, the sports magazine with the largest circulation in Germany, ran a feature on "our legionnaires on the island" for all those readers curious to find out whether the exports were now addicted to brown sauce and cribbage, and to chuckle at the funny folk who drink tea and eat jam sandwiches made out of that floppy white bread at four o'clock in the afternoon. It was like reading a love letter written by John Major to Roy Hattersley.

People began to realise that Newcastle is not merely a destination for ferries leaving Hamburg, started scouring their road maps for the whereabouts of Derby and finally found out that the Anfield Red Machine has ground to a halt. They even stopped tagging an "S" on to the end of Tottenham Hotspur (although the habit of referring to "Arsenal London", "Manchester" and, distressingly, "FC Everton Liverpool", is still alive, kicking and causing sensitive ears to bleed). The lure of your Italys and Spains, which had ensnared three genera-tions of German footballer, from Netzer to Bierhoff, had been not so much pushed on the back-burner as shoved violently into oblivion behind the cooker.

Throughout most of the season, it was easy to recognise ex-pats inter-ested in football. They were the ones who had grown a foot taller, or who were strutting around with pride-swollen chests and hubristic sneers, or who drummed their fingers at the sheer tedium of having to sit through the televised highlights of the Bundesliga.

However, unless one is a proponent of the Ken Bailey way of doing things, taking an inordinate amount of pride in your country is not really the sort of character trait which gains you anything except a close-up view of the breadth of other people's backs. Gratitude should therefore be expressed to an acquaintance of mine for giving it from the shoulder: the Germans playing in the British leagues in 1998-99, he reckoned, were no good anyway.

He compared them to canned mushrooms, which, in Germany, have clear-cut lines of demarcation. *Erste Wahl* (first choice) are so pristine, so perfectly contoured, that you want to eschew popping them into your mouth in favour of accompanying them arm-in-arm on a long, leafy walk on Clapham Common. *Zweite Wahl* (second choice) have the texture and taste of a mollusc with an over-active sebaceous gland, and *dritte Wahl* (third choice) are so aesthetically displeasing as to resemble Christian Ziege with a Beatles haircut. But the German players in England, he instructed, were fourth choice, and that doesn't even exist. They were the fungus, puffballs, the empty can chucked into the dustbin, he cackled.

As the pectorals shrank from Bluto to Olive Oyl and the grin turned to that of the cat who had got a backside full of buckshot rather than a saucer full of cream, the ex-pat was forced to look the truth full in the face. Despite their talents of sorts, all the Germans who had come over lacked the specialness of their predecessors, be it the zest of Klinsmann, the courage of Trautmann or the fell-asleep-on-the-night-bus surliness of Eike Immel.

Stefan Schnoor at Derby, despite losing his hair with a degree of suaveness not seen in British sport since Graham Gooch opened for England, still toddled about like any of the other the odd-toed ungulates who play in his position up and down the country. You had Steffen Freund at Spurs, whose impressive reviews belied the suspicion that he could be replaced by any number of hand-held gardening implements if only they could learn to stick their foot in and not shy away from a booking or two. Stefan Klos aroused immediate suspicion that he had emigrated solely because of his surname (translatable as "khazis"). Sean Dundee, wunderkind-by-passport, who had one good season at Karlsruhe and then gadded his Bundesliga career away in the balmy nightspots of Baden, tempted providence among the hipsters and flipsters of the Liverpool dressing-room by wearing an earring in both ears.

Even the better ones must have been sold as seen without anybody seeing enough, or at the right time. Karl-Heinz Riedle, for example, although displaying the distended cranium of Joe Royle, would have to scour the microfiche at the library to discover the last reference to him as "Air Riedle" that wasn't accompanied by an ironic snigger. And back home in Bavaria, Didi Hamman, arguably the best of the lot and widely touted as one of the most velvety midfield schemers in England, was what the Germans call the "water-carrier" for the ball players in Bayern Munich's creative department.

They had hoodwinked us once again. The very few British players who have made their mark in the Bundesliga – Keegan, Alan McInally, Paul Lambert and even the medusan Neil Marmon in the lower leagues – were bought for a specific quality that wasn't particularly abundant on German soil at that specific club at that specific time (the fact that this quality was usually either "scampering around" or "dishing it out" is neither here nor there).

However, the British-based German class of 1998-99 were dispatched because their paymasters knew they wouldn't be needed at home and, moreover, that they would be wanted in Britain. And thus German bank accounts increased, more money was ploughed into importing real exotics into the Bundesliga – Lizarazu, Scandinavians with tattoos, what seemed like half of the Brazilian B team – and the ex-pats continued to have their hair ruffled in public houses when football was on the television.

Any amount of skulduggery cannot, of course, disguise the fact that this season's Champions League final featured a British team triumphing over a German team. It is impossible not to admire Manchester United's never-say-die attitude. It would be indecorous in the extreme to begrudge pundits the chance to wheel out Gary Lineker's *bon mot* about football and 22 men and Germans always winning. And only those who have never loved could fail to have been stirred by Teddy Sheringham's celebrations, with his crinkly eyes and little dimples and that.

The final two minutes, as *Schadenfreude* kicked off its shoes in its own living room after the commentator's voice had been all of a sing-song, and he'd started referring to the players by their forename only and informing us what they would be doing on the streets of Munich later on that evening, were worth any number of Warhol's famous 15, as were the close-ups of Franz Beckenbauer, crestfallen and looking for somebody to blame. It would have been positively schoolmasterly to rebuke those who momentarily clambered up onto the nearest rooftop and shouted about their country's footballing superiority to anybody who would listen.

However, a wagging index finger of restraint is one of the keys to social acceptance in Germany. Beckenbauer and his sidekick Uli Hoeness may be as attractive as a stagnant pond, but their string-pulling and gamesmanship mean they are also just as transparent. In fact, it wouldn't be at all surprising if they lost it on purpose, just to make the British leagues even more appealing for the hordes of cloggers at home.

But it won't be Jancker or Jeremies or Zickler or any of the others with a future who will be upping sticks and swapping their felt hats and *Lederhosen* for a Robin Asquith haircut and those Britpop trousers which make your arse disappear. It will be people like Markus Babbel or Mario Basler, who, at the time of writing, are being linked with Newcastle. A starched-hipped defender and a tab-smoking, beer-swilling maverick the wrong side of 30 who is good at free kicks would hardly be a rarity in a Newcastle team, but they'll probably come – or if not them, then someone like them – and they'll love it and they'll enrich nothing and nobody except themselves.

And this will more than likely go on in 1999-2000 and every other season until the end of the next millennium. But not one of the Baslers or Babbels will spare a thought for those of us who travelled in the opposite direction and now find ourselves condemned to peals of malicious laughter for the rest of our lives, simply because British chairmen fancy a bit of European. Let me take your coat, *Weltschmerz*, you're probably stopping longer.

dens fog
gary oliver

Dundee surprised everyone by avoiding relegation and exposed the true face of the Scottish Premier League in the process. It wasn't a pretty sight

Throughout season 1998-99 Rangers and Celtic swatted aside all league opposition, regularly racking up five goals or more. And Scottish football was at sixes and sevens off the park as well, its confusion due entirely to fallout from the new Scottish Premier League.

For many years Scotland's leading sides had agitated for autonomy. By the mid-1980s voting power had become loaded in favour of the larger clubs yet still the top league kept alive the myth (and cliche) that the tail was wagging the dog. Consequently, the Premier Division beast became increasingly disloyal to its 100-year-old master, the Scottish Football League.

Covetously eyeing the English Premiership, in 1992 ten clubs formed the company Scottish Super League – a title naff and inappropriate in equal measure. Intended to be a franchise operation, the putative super league affronted those still clinging to the quaint notion that football leagues ought to be meritocratic. There was considerable *Schadenfreude*, therefore, when Dunfermline, St Johnstone, Dundee United, Partick and Hibernian – half the original, self-styled elite – each subsequently did penance in the lower leagues.

However, it had taken an unexpected handbrake turn by Celtic, then controlled by the discredited Kelly and White dynasties, for the SSL mission to be aborted. And although the Scottish Football League was reorganised into four divisions of ten in 1994, few believed that the moratorium on further change would be respected for the agreed five years. Sure enough, in September 1997, at the fag end of both the existing TV contracts and the four-year title sponsorship by Bell's Distillers, the then Premier Division resigned *en masse* from the Scottish League.

For the clubs involved, the self-governing Premiership was to be a cash-rich, footballing Elysium; those excluded could go hang. Not surprisingly, the remnant of the Scottish League was, initially, near unanimous in its hostility. Eventually, however, the minnows were bought off, while a guarantee to expand the new league to at least 12 teams placated enough clubs higher up the food chain.

First to break ranks and defect to the rebel camp had been Raith Rovers and Dundee. Both were motivated by self-interest. Raith had been one of the original conspirators prior to their relegation, while Dundee regarded themselves as champions-elect of the First Division. The Taysiders' confidence proved to be justified and in 1998 they stepped up to become members of the inaugural SPL. Having helped oil the breakaway, owners Jimmy and Peter Marr might have expected that their back-scratching would be reciprocated. But throughout 1998-99 Dundee's new playmates showed them little gratitude.

Teams supported the SPL in expectation of various windfalls, satellite TV to be the principal cash cow. Little did Dundee suspect that as the league's newcomers they were, for spurious reasons, to receive a less than equitable share of Murdoch's millions. For the brothers Marr it was a shock slap in the face, particularly when Hibernian, whom Dundee had replaced, were in receipt of a "golden parachute" to cushion their landing in the First Division.

An equally contentious issue involving Dundee, but with far wider implications, was the mandatory refurbishment of Dens Park. Remarkable though it now seems, Dens regularly staged cup semi-finals, housing 15-20,000 crowds, right through the 1980s. Only ten years later, the SPL considered it unfit even for routine fixtures. There was no denying that Dens Park was the Premier League's sore thumb. Home fans had for 20 years risked piles and splinters from the exposed benches bolted on to ancient terracing. Visiting supporters continued to stand, enduring a quite appalling view from their shallow, open terrace. Dundee were granted one year in which to give the division's ugliest ground a 10,000-seat makeover, to be complete by July 31st, 1999.

For a club trying to reverse a generation of precipitous decline, financing a £3 million project was no formality. Fund-raising schemes ranged from the mundane, such as asking fans to pay £25 for a brick, to the surreal, like seeking investment from Giovanni di Stefano, the businessman who also acts as "foreign spokesman" for a Serbian paramilitary group. At a time when NATO was poised to launch air strikes against Yugoslavia – a subject on which Di Stefano naturally offered trenchant views – Dundee's choice of benefactor was, to say the least, ill-advised. It also confirmed just how desperate for cash the club was.

Vice-chairman Derek Soutar promised to quit if the Italian came aboard, but still the Marr brothers did not sever the link. Di Stefano continued to provide soundbites such as: "I could write my knowledge of football on a postage stamp and still have space to write a protest to Clinton about NATO air strike policy."

His black humour did not amuse a Premier League which was already gunning for Dundee. One of BSkyB's earliest broadcasts was of St Johnstone's visit to Dens Park. Viewers nationwide witnessed an appalling match, played in a sodden, rundown stadium before a minuscule crowd, much of which was out of camera shot. For a new organisation anxious to establish its credentials, there could not have been a worse advertisement.

Consequently, the SPL's chief executive Roger Mitchell appeared indifferent to his member club's obvious difficulties. The mid-Atlantic Mitchell is obsessed by spectator demographics and rickety old Dens Park is presumably thought to be the kind of habitat populated by too many of the "35-year-old, working-class males" whom he holds in such obvious disdain. Mitchell maintained there could be no compromise and threatened, *ad nauseam*, that unless Dens Park was satisfactorily revamped and open for business by July 31st, Dundee would be kicked out of the top division.

Mitchell may have thought his warning hypothetical, since pre-season expectation had been that Dundee would finish bottom and go down in the conventional manner. Much to the critics' chagrin, however, the workaday team failed to oblige, leaving Dunfermline, Hearts and neighbours United to dispute tenth position. As the season progressed, however, there grew a belief that the bottom club would be spared relegation, with Dundee instead being cast back into the SFL. As late as March 23rd, with Dens Park still intact, the Scottish *Daily Express* reported breathlessly: "Dundee have failed in a desperate double bid to secure a groundshare deal for the start of next season, which will lead to them being kicked out of the Scottish Premier League and throw a sensational lifeline to struggling clubs such as Hearts and Dunfermline."

The *Express* – "Official Partner of the Scottish Premier League", interestingly – described its story as an exclusive, yet it contained nothing surprising. Many fans were by then already taking the view that the final league placings would most likely count for nothing. As Dundee's board continued to rummage down sofas for money, apparently with little success, that notion understandably gathered pace. Moreover, the SPL did and said nothing to halt its momentum. The wonder was that anyone was still bothering to attend the so-called relegation battles.

Not until early April, after months of misleading speculation, did the SPL contradict received wisdom: "Our rules state that the club finishing bottom will be relegated," confirmed SPL administrator Ian

Blair. "Dundee could have been expelled through default, although I've no idea what the Scottish Football League would have said in the event of two teams dropping down."

That statement came after Dundee had assured the other nine clubs that funding for the two new stands was in place. Erecting them was scheduled to take 16 weeks. By mid-April, therefore, when the bulldozers moved in, Dundee were already playing catch-up. And with the club's fate seemingly in the hands of Barr Construction, the portents were not good. In recent summers, similar projects by the same company for Dunfermline and Raith Rovers had taken much longer and in both cases it had been September before the revamped stadiums were fully operational.

Moreover, some reports intimated that only divine intervention could keep the Dark Blues playing at all. Throughout the season there was much talk of a merger with – or, to be more accurate, takeover by – Dundee United. Every denial from Dens was at least slightly ambiguous, with Dundee's directors thought eager to rid themselves of the millstone around their necks. No sooner were the bulldozers and hard hats on site than the *Express* – the SPL's "official partner" remember – ran a damaging front page lead that stated unequivocally: "Dundee Football Club will be taken over and closed down by arch rivals Dundee United at the end of the season... it is understood an announcement confirming the demise of the Dens Park side will be made within the next two weeks."

"Absolute rubbish," was the retort by chairman Jimmy Marr. "We've just signed a £3.5 million contract and work has already started. We wouldn't be doing this if we were about to sell the club in two weeks' time." Perhaps not. Yet doubters continued to question whether the demolition would necessarily be followed by any construction. And the sceptics seemed to include even Dundee's manager, Jocky Scott. "Once we see the steel being erected we will know the club is going places and all the doubts will vanish," he said. "I can only go on what I'm told."

Not exactly a ringing endorsement of his board. The contractors remained upbeat, vowing that they would give 110 per cent in trying to meet the July 31st deadline. Yet still the SPL warned that Dundee could "expel themselves" on that date. Where that would then leave the Premier and First divisions was anyone's guess. Fans were left to conclude, therefore, that either the SPL enjoys making empty threats or else Scotland's leagues faced probable chaos on the eve of a new season.

The latter seemed entirely possible, the Premier League having relished any opportunity to undermine the remnant of the Scottish League. The new body's first act had been to unilaterally scrap the promotion play-off between the club finishing second bottom of the Premier League and the First Division runners-up. Falkirk, who finished second in 1998, were instead bunged a measly £250,000. And whereas Dundee were at least granted a year in which to sort themselves out, Premier League wannabes must now comply with the door policy before winning the First Division title. In other words, a club's status in Scottish football is no longer determined solely by its achievements on the park.

The implications were clear even as Hibernian ran away with the First Division title, allowing the Premier League to welcome home its favoured son. For while the Edinburgh side clearly boasted the most impressive squad, Hibs also had an incentive denied their challengers. Before Christmas 1998, Roger Mitchell had announced that Falkirk and Ayr, then in close contention, would be refused promotion to the SPL. Small wonder, then, that soon afterwards the erstwhile contenders allowed Hibs to gallop over the horizon.

Ayr United's predicament was particularly curious since chairman Bill Barr owns the company that has thrown up new stands throughout Scotland. Still terraced on three sides, thirty-something fans grew up believing Ayr's ground was known as "trim" Somerset Park.

A generation later, it seems compulsory for all visiting journalists to sneer at what is now regarded as a museum piece. And yet in January 1999, Somerset Park was still allowed to accommodate over 10,000 spectators for a Scottish Cup victory over neighbours Kilmarnock. The pitch and facilities are also of a sufficient standard for the national team to prepare there. Why such a venue cannot also house the four or five thousand who would attend routine SPL fixtures remains an insoluble riddle.

Ayr and Falkirk, along with Morton and Hamilton, are actively trying to relocate. But Mitchell also insists the SPL will not countenance temporary ground sharing – despite the precedent of Celtic renting Hampden Park in the mid-Nineties, having failed to comply in time with the Taylor Report. Furthermore, no sooner had the demolition of Dens Park begun than it was speculated Dundee might begin the following season playing at Airdrie, 70-odd miles away. Member clubs can, it seems, vote to break Mitchell's dictum. Why might it be acceptable for a team to decant for a month but not a season? Answers on a postcard, please, to Ayr United and Falkirk.

But then the Premier League gods have always acted in mysterious ways. The body purports to be a model of democracy, yet steadfastly avoids public scrutiny of its practices. For instance, the Scottish League clubs waved through the breakaway on the understanding that from season 2000-01 the SPL would comprise at least 12 teams. The new league had pledged to confirm details of the enlargement before Christmas, but time and again the announcement was deferred without explanation.

In March the reason became clear when it was revealed that the country's smallest clubs had been discussing a trade-off that might allow the Premier League to continue with only ten teams. Understandably, that collusion had the aspirant First Division clubs seething, leading to speculation that they themselves might desert the Scottish League out of pique to become SPL part two – a U-turn that would be akin to Mirror Group pensioners asking the Maxwell brothers to administer their affairs.

The months of prevarication left Scottish League clubs drumming their fingers, unable to confirm any reorganisation of their own. Not until April did the SPL finally give its written guarantee that a 12-team league would be forthcoming. But as sceptics continued to point out, there is little to prevent Premier sides wriggling out of this, or any other, commitment. Accountable to no one, the top division can act however and at whatever pace it chooses, with every other club then expected to fall into line. The only brake that can be applied to the SPL juggernaut is the threat of being disowned by the Scottish FA and that scenario was made even more unlikely by the removal of its combative chief executive Jim Farry in March.

Before the 1997 schism, the Scottish Football League had already dictated that by the first season of the new millennium there would be similar criteria for stadia in its top division. It was fair to assume, however, that their more benign regime would have supported clubs who were making genuine attempts to comply. The SPL, by contrast, wields its rule book as a blunt instrument: "Clubs have 15 months to shape up before 2000-01," Mitchell warned in January 1999. "If they don't, they can forget it."

And for the most hard-pressed team of all, the day of reckoning would arrive much sooner. The demolition of Dens Park was under way, the players had ensured they would not finish bottom (indeed they finally finished fifth) and still Roger Mitchell chanted his mantra, "The work has to be completed by 31st July or Dundee will have expelled themselves from the SPL." Small wonder, then, that when Dundee defeated Kilmarnock 2-1 on April 24th, climbing into the top half of the table, what remained of Dens Park resonated to the defiant chant of "Are you watching, SPL?".

That late surge quietened the critics. And events elsewhere also helped take the heat off Dundee. Conspicuously silent following the mayhem, both on and off the field, which accompanied Rangers' victory at Celtic Park on May 2nd, a discomfited SPL judiciously dropped the charge that Dundee's association with Giovanni di Stefano had brought the league into disrepute.

And so the season ended with no one knowing for sure which sides would participate in the next Premier League. "If Dundee are having difficulties meeting the deadline and plan a groundshare for next season, they have to let us know," Mitchell insisted. "We would expect to hear from them by no later than early June... it is our intention to carry out our own assessment of work and an independent audit."

But by then bewildered fans had conducted their own audit of the 1998-99 season – and found that the machinations of the Scottish Premier League simply did not add up.

turning point
steve parish

Thousands of Man City fans walked out of their most important game of the season with minutes to go, then wished they hadn't

"Where were you when Kennedy was shot?" is just a question. It does not imply suspicion that you might have been the second gunman. But for Manchester City fans, five years from now, seated in the new stadium, watching City in European competition, "Where were you when Dickov scored?" will hang around some people's necks like a placard of shame. Their crime, their enduring guilt, will be lack of faith, allied to the knowledge that they missed what would have been one of the best moments of their lives.

They are the ones who were streaming away from Wembley when City went 1-0 down to Gillingham in the 80th minute of the 1999 Second Division play-off final, or, if not then, when Gillingham scored again in the 85th. Most, maybe as many as 5,000, turned around and were readmitted to watch extra time after City equalised. Cars were abandoned in the road, Wembley Park's platforms emptied. One man is reported to have pulled the emergency handle on a departing train and run back up the track. Noel Gallagher turned the limo round; Liam hadn't left but was already in the executive bar.

A few did not turn. A "portly" man who didn't fancy the long walk back to the stadium just carried on to the tube and the car at the other end. Others had already joined the ticketless ones in pubs to watch while some of the ticketless ones went to the stadium and got in. Others couldn't face the thought of going back to perhaps yet another twist of the knife.

Some had been persuaded to leave early by family or friends. Friendships, marriages, may never recover. Reluctant children were shepherded away by the same parents who had taught them that being a City supporter was different, character-building, but who had, finally, given up hope.

But let's face it, we all had. Even when Kevin Horlock scored the consolation goal with 20 seconds left of the 90 minutes, it was just going to be another act of false-dawn cruelty, and the final chorus of "We love you City, we do" just another defiant declaration of our irrational affection. Few of us saw the fourth official hold up the board for five minutes added time; the Wembley scoreboard stood fixed at 90. Gillingham fans had been whistling for time since the 88th minute, but now hardly dare sing "You're not singing any more", the only football song most of them seemed to know.

Then, with 94 minutes gone, the ball breaks to Paul Dickov, already denied a goal by the leg of Gills' goalie Vince Bartram, his mate from Arsenal days and best man at his wedding. Dickov shoots, maybe gets a slight deflection off a defender's shin, and the ball sails majestically over man-of-the-match Bartram (a case of premature annunciation) and hits the back of the net. There is a brief second of mass disbelief, momentary denial that City have come back from the dead, then bedlam breaks out.

Two more minutes of time play out, with what's happening on the pitch almost a blur. I go to the toilet. Behind the stand there is a stream of people going one way. I'm confused. "Where are you going? Don't you realise there's extra time?" Then it dawns on me – these are the disappeared, the ones who left, the faithless who have already suffered their time in purgatory because they were not there, making their way back to their seats (except the bloke behind me who wrecked his before he went) and hoping that eventual bliss will be theirs.

Extra time passes quickly, everyone at the City end standing throughout. City's defence offers the sort of opportunity that led to the Gills' goals, but real chances are few. Looming ominously is the pre-season's favourite prediction, that City would fight back to equalise in the play-off final then lose on penalties. Nicky Weaver, City's young goalie, has never saved a penalty, while City's list of crucial missed spot-kicks is a long one.

The penalties are to be at the City end and it's City to go first. Horlock steps up. There is some whistling from the far end, but he tucks it away. As the first Gillingham player places the ball, a cacophony of whistling, of Health-and-Safety warning proportions, rises from the City end of the ground. Weaver takes off to his right, the shot goes down the middle, but he still manages to stick out his leg and knock it away. Hero Dickov is next, but his shot bounces off both posts and out.

For Gillingham's next, the whistling creates a vacuum and the ball is sucked wide of the post. 1-0 after four penalties. Terry Cooke tucks his into the corner. Gillingham score theirs. Edghill hammers his first-ever goal for City in off the bar. And Weaver beats out Gillingham's fourth attempt, beckons his team-mates, then sets off on a glorious chase round the back of the goal, along the running track and back on to the pitch finally to be caught and buried under the team.

I'm hugging my 19-year-old son, on whom I have inflicted this passion, and who – apart from when we tanked United 5-1 – has known only struggle and despair. The celebrations turn to song, including a heartfelt rendition of *The Great Escape*, as the Gillingham end empties except for the couple of hundred City fans who hid their colours and got in and stayed.

The team throw shoes and other bits of kit to the crowd, then get down on their knees and do a "We are not worthy" prostration to the fans on the three sides, then at last turn to acknowledge the huddled few at the corner of the now-deserted far end, most of whom have paid well over the odds from the touts and "ticket agencies". The PA stops its choice of music long enough for us to sing *Blue Moon*.

For those who were there, the chaos over the ticketing was forgotten. It was expected from previous play-offs that allocation would reflect average home gates, but Gillingham's Scally-by-name, scally-by-nature chairman persuaded the League to let them have 35,000 tickets – five times the average gate at Priestfield – on the grounds that "there was massive interest in Kent". Well, yes, from Man Utd and Arsenal supporters for whom Gillingham was "their second team" or people who had never been to a match before. The police had not been consulted, and it was expected that a lot of tickets would go to touts and on to City fans.

With threats of expulsion for people in the wrong end and most tickets having gone to people willing to support Gillingham for the day, there were no more than a few hundred City fans amid the brand new dark blue shirts and jester hats. But you only needed a Medway address to get eight tickets (before the League cut it to a mere four) and all the Gillingham tickets were sold within one and half days – so fast that some season ticket holders failed to get theirs. Up at Maine Road, the terms "brewery", "piss-up" and "organise" were in common use as the club attempted to shift its 39,000 tickets (average gate 28,000), while satisfying the needs of 14,000 season ticket holders and 5,000 members.

Most City fans who made it to Wembley didn't seem to begrudge the Gills their day out. If you had queued for 12 hours at Maine Road, or spent hours trying to get through on the phoneline, or paid over £100 for an £18 ticket, the victory would make it worthwhile. On the other hand, if you were one of the regulars at home and away matches without either a season ticket or membership card, and had lost your place in the sun to someone from Kent who just fancied a day out, or if you were the frail old lady who collapsed within sight of the Maine Road ticket office after all day and half the evening in a queue, or if you were one of the staff who worked over 16 hours selling tickets (finishing the first day at ten past midnight), you might get a different view of what is fair.

I was put in mind of Bill Tidy's famous cartoon in *Foul* of a couple decked out for the Henley regatta, trying to punt up Wembley Way, with a real fan grumbling "Come Cup final day, and it's a bleedin' social occasion." For the staunch Gills fans, it might have been easier to get behind their team if they had not been surrounded by 25,000 people who didn't really care. Galling, too, to lose like that and then have some fair-weather supporter say, "Well, it's only a game."

Still, they filled their end, and the familiar cry of "You couldn't sell all your tickets" was silenced. One little highlight was the sight of the Gillingham players trudging to the tunnel but applauding the City supporters as they went, cementing a mutual respect between the two teams and their supporters. It was a shame we then had the nonsense from Scally, demanding a replay because the match referee, staying in the Wembley Hilton, found himself that evening among City fans who honoured him with a chant of thanks for the five minutes of time added on.

Outside Wembley, with most Gillingham fans long gone, Wembley Park station had a signal failure. City fans stood, largely silent, exhausted. Someone posted on an on-line fanzine that "this is the way Kurt Cobain dreamed people would leave his shows". It was indeed a sort of Nirvana, a serenity far removed from the turmoil of the last hours – or indeed the last nine months, the last four years.

I'd been to more away matches this season than since 1974. I left the railways then and the cost and time involved in going away confined trips to local derbies or cup matches. This year, the under-£10 pricing for most away games and the prospect of a regular lift got me back in the routine. I even decided to go to some matches at the last minute and bought tickets outside.

Fulham – one of the "big" matches – meant a haul down the M6 and the M40, a scenic route through Richmond Park, and an hour by the Thames watching the tide change. York and Lincoln, pleasant trips despite the results, were offset by having to visit the slum grounds of Wigan and Blackpool, and having the Staffordshire police at Stoke trying to impose martial law because a few people wouldn't sit down. The thought of having to go back to the New Den was probably a major incentive for one last effort at Wembley. Now at last we can get back to Blackburn and Wolves (and Crewe) and no doubt be fleeced again by Forest.

The sold-out signs will be much needed at Maine Road. Incredibly, more people watched City v Burnley in 1998-99 than in the old First Division in 1973 with a forward line of Summerbee, Bell, Marsh and Lee. There was a theory that City fans' booing of poor play (and barracking of individual players) was not just counter-productive, but was actually attracting crowds of people who liked a good moan. The Maine Road faithful were often worth a goal – to the opposition. It took the players half a season to adjust to the Second Division, but the fans never did.

I repeated in the local press a tale (rumours were what the *Evening News* asked for) that during half-time the City team just sat around in silence; it wasn't true, but it was credible because the will to compete was just not there. "No early passion" said one visiting manager, as City took it easy once more against another team eager to make it their "cup final" – a cliche that the City fans only encouraged with chants of "1-0 in your cup final" whenever we managed to take the lead. At one stage, the signs of depression were looking desperately like the year before.

Then in October Andy Morrison arrived for £80,000 from Huddersfield. Apart from always being favourite to get the defensive header out, here was someone who very obviously minded if he lost – on one occasion picking up a bench and hurling it down the players' tunnel. The transformation in the team meant that suddenly automatic promotion looked a possibility. Defeat at home by Oldham and Wycombe, and Walsall's refusal to crack under the pressure, led instead to Wembley.

Some supporters are now seriously pondering whether two relegations and three seasons of dross were worthwhile in order to enjoy those moments at Wembley. They would be the ones who wanted an open-top bus for the team through the streets of Manchester for coming third in the old Third Division. Perhaps not, but it does seem City fans are happier about that achievement than United fans are about the Treble. The difference is that United have bought their satisfaction, whereas at City we've had to wait until the old lady feels like it. And that's true love.

old habits die
ken sproat

A tempestuous and bitter relationship
between a fan and his club ended in
divorce – and relief

Some people have a personal motto. Mine is: "If it's
more hassle than it's worth, don't do it." This theory
is fine when procrastinating about hanging wallpaper,
but less easily applied when it comes to an obsession.

In the past, everything has had to come a poor second to the overriding
priority of attending Newcastle United matches. Absolutely nothing
would get in my way. I've turned down good jobs rather than risk
working a Saturday afternoon. Weddings, holidays and personal responsibilities have been organised to avoid clashing with games. Yet somehow
there has been a gradual slackening in the intensity of our relationship, a relationship in which I have been taken for granted but in which
I was prepared to give unconditional loyalty and forgiveness.

The reasons for the cooling are manifold. I could elucidate several
key moments that shook me from my NUFC tree, such as the pain in
the neck spoilt brat I had to sit beside on a Bulgarian hydrofoil in the
Keegan years. Newcastle had just been christened "The Entertainers"

and my fellow traveller was wearing a Newcastle top. He was from Surrey. The realisation hit me that Newcastle were not an entity personal to me and 25,000 other Geordies any more. They were a nationally marketed product.

Call it snobbery, but I've never been one for popular causes. I was always the first to champion a rock group, then disown them when they got into the charts. For something to be real it has to be personal. Personal things do not come off the shelf in handy packages. You have to put lots of effort into it, preferably suffering greatly along the way. Extreme, but that's me.

The club itself has been doing everything possible to make me hate them, but then they always had. The difference now is that it costs ten times as much and I was being threatened with eviction if I didn't like it. "There is a waiting list of 10,000 who would be grateful for your seat," was a regular theme in the local press. On the field the team were hitting new peaks but I just wasn't connecting. The feeling of thrashing opponents wasn't as good as I thought it would be. The pain of defeat was always more intense than the pleasure of victory and I think I must have suffered a footballing emotional breakdown when Newcastle threw the league title away in 1996.

Fellow supporters became insufferable. They harangued the team under Keegan, so imagine how sour and hateful the atmosphere became under Dalglish. Terrible, dark, secret thoughts started to creep into my mind. I began to want the opposition to score, just to sicken the fans around me. "That'll teach 'em," my indignant alter ego would rejoice to itself. Despite all this, I've kept going to all the home matches (away games simply became impossibly expensive), spending money I could barely afford watching matches I was getting nothing from, surrounded mostly by people I abhor. The inevitable crunch came during the 1998-99 season.

Newcastle games have long been unmemorable. Sitting in the same place, "tetty fields" from the pitch, watching seemingly identical matches somewhat strips a game of its individuality. The season turns into a flick through holiday photographs, a blur of half-remembered disjointed occurrences. The thrill goes and suddenly you are wondering why you are messing around with your life and the lives of your family just to take part in the bitter circus of the Premier League and then sit in interminable queues of traffic.

The intense radio phone-in recriminations point fingers at the relentless injustice of the football universe. Meanwhile, you sit gripping the steering wheel, seething because deep inside you know you have wasted a day doing something you will have forgotten by Monday morning. The feeling is made worse because you cannot admit to yourself that you didn't want to do it in the first place.

This contradiction has been building inside me for at least five years, slipping from my subconscious into my conscious being with subversive stealth. But again and again I would deny it. For to admit as much would, in a way, mean owning up to having wasted my life and to have been wrong to relegate my non-footballing responsibilities for 25 years.

The cliche about TV programmes spoiling the adverts applies to me. My life has been a long pause between football matches. It has been a very painful personal journey and a lot of soul searching ensued when logic kept telling me what I really wanted was to quit. As soon as I resolved to stop going to Newcastle games the weight of my history, of the investment of time, money and emotion I had made in them would prevent me from taking the big step. Time and again I would renew my season ticket.

The internal debate about my continued presence at St James' Park was complicated by the fact that for the past ten years I have gone to Newcastle games with my wife. These are "our" times when we do something just for ourselves, our nights out, our time to be alone together. A strange concept when 36,000 other people are there, but I'm sure you know what I mean. To stop going to the games could possibly damage our marriage too.

Another facet of my football persona is the love of Blyth Spartans and Bedlington Terriers. Until this season it hasn't been a problem and I have operated the strict personal pecking order of Newcastle, Blyth, Bedlington. Blyth Spartans could look after themselves if I was at St James' because they have always been relatively strong and well supported. The Terriers were a rather interesting if shambolic diversion and all three clubs existed in totally different orbits. I never missed a Newcastle match to attend another. My monogamy was pure.

In contrast to the ridiculous intensity of the Premier League, the non-League scene is a genuine pleasure. The standard of football obviously isn't as good. But excitement doesn't necessarily depend on good football. On Easter Monday I attended Bedlington v Morpeth, Gateshead v Blyth and Newcastle v Tottenham in that order. The games got worse as the day progressed.

Other than the technical aspects of the match itself, everything is better on the non-League scene. The prices, the freedom, the frequency of bizarre happenings, the lack of chest-beating triumphalism and a brow-beating boardroom. In short, I'm wanted and I feel comfortable with the morality. In my experience, the further up the football structure you go, the more fans are perceived as pests.

Bedlington Terriers were about as low as organised football can get but I grew to love my visits to their Doctor Pit Welfare ground. Then over the years they got better. A lot better. The problem was, as they got better, their orbit started to wander and they began to cross into territories previously considered impossible to visit. The first clash within my world order was when Bedlington played Blyth in an FA Cup match. I stood at the back of the stand, a forlorn, haunted and pitiful wreck. It was as if my two best friends were trying to murder each other. Each goal was a stab to the heart, whoever scored.

The Terriers went from strength to strength and as I had invested heavily (on an emotional basis) in their recent history so I was inevitably drawn along with them. In the 1998-99 season they surpassed it all and embarked on one of those once-in-a-lifetime FA Cup journeys. On November 14th, 1998 they played Colchester United in the first round proper. Sheffield Wednesday were to play at Newcastle on the same day. The crunch had come.

Days of anguish followed. The conflict invaded my sleep. Long, frank discussions took place with work colleagues and within the family. I went for lengthy, solitary, storm-blasted walks along the beach. I suppose the conclusion was inevitable although the execution was not. Bedlington needed me that day, Newcastle did not. Eventually, after rehearsing the line over and over, I plucked up the courage to say to my wife: "Tell your brother he can have my ticket for the Sheff Wed game. I'm going to Bedlington." She understood. Oh, the relief. Only then did I know I had done what was correct.

Folklore will tell how Bedlington thrashed Colchester. Generations to come will learn of that match. I'll have to remind most of you that Newcastle and Sheffield Wednesday drew 1-1. An insipid mess by all accounts.

Of course, I still possess my Newcastle season ticket and vowed I wouldn't miss another Toon game all season. So what do Bedlington do? Get to the FA Vase semi-final, which is to be played the same day as Newcastle are to host Manchester United. This choice was a lot easier once I reminded myself that the opposition is irrelevant. If I was to go to St James' Park it was to watch Newcastle, not Man United. Bedlington won 5-0 and I was there. Newcastle lost and I didn't have to suffer watching the Reds celebrating or the Newcastle fans' overbearing belligerence. To tell the truth I didn't even have to think about that match at all. It's as if it happened in a different galaxy.

In their unblinking logic and wisdom the FA scheduled the FA Vase final for the same day as the concluding Premier League matches. Newcastle v Blackburn or my team at Wembley? Anguish didn't come into it any more. I was off to Wembley.

Meanwhile, Newcastle went on a little cup run of their own. If I had thought I had been feeling numb towards them then the tension that racked my body during the semi-final against Spurs came as a real shock. The old feelings came back but again, it wasn't the thrill of winning I felt but the intestine-churning anxiety. Being able to relax at 2-0 up merely prevented me from vomiting. It must have been a good match for this to happen. For me, success is measured in being able to keep my dinner down. I love Newcastle United but I hate them. This is what they do to me.

The 1998-99 FA Vase final and the 1998-99 FA Cup final. Both on the same ground on consecutive weeks. The former featuring Bedlington Terriers, the latter a sullied cash cow called Newcastle United. Has fate ever created such a grotesque laboratory for a man to experiment with his displaced and fractured loyalty?

My head was swimming with a tangle of emotions leading up to the fateful week. Arrogantly, I suppose, and stupidly, I thought a Terriers Vase victory was a historical inevitability. To me it was the perfect final – the holders versus the non-League team of the season and the justifying apex of a lifelong effort of watching football. Half of the population of Bedlington journeyed to Wembley. For every regular attender at a normal game, 25 had gone to London. I sat away from them. This was to be my personal moment of sheer, untainted, unashamed glory.

But Tiverton scored the only goal with 17 seconds remaining – a miscued shot trickling past the stranded keeper at one mile an hour. It barely reached the back of the net. I slumped sideways, my legs of jelly unwilling and unable to move, which was bad, seeing as I suddenly and very urgently needed to go to the toilet. I rushed to the gents, vomited half a pound of wine gums, then stormed out of Wembley at the final whistle, face like a smacked backside. Why me? My desperate, illogical thought processes worked it out: "I know, it's to enable a Newcastle victory next week!"

Back to London six days later and I had sort-of convinced myself that Newcastle could beat Man Utd. As ever, as with all aspects of my life, I travelled incognito. In the ultra tense hour before kick-off a drunken, eyes-rolling-independently Newcastle fan accused me of being a Man Utd fan.

"Anybody can wear a shirt bonny lad. It's what's inside that matters," I menaced in reply, my accent disarming his assumption. As I took my seat, probably due to the drunk, my conscience was yelling "Ken, you are a hypocrite" at the part of my brain that was flooded with adrenalin. Confusion reigned but I wanted and needed a Newcastle victory. This was to be my last game as a regular and I wanted, like a retiring player, to go out on a high. As the players came out of the tunnel I said to my wife: "It has to be. And it will be. For me." Her furrowed brow was the perfect riposte.

At ten past three Sheringham scored and my world caved in. As the game progressed Newcastle were letting me down. Each mistake compounded my frustration. Still I hoped. Scholes scored. Two-nil. How brilliant it will be when we win from here. Ketsbaia hits the post. Come on, we can still do it. Ten minutes left, Maric rolls it wide.

That was it. Years of frustration exploded from my normally polite mouth. The unreleased anger following the Bedlington defeat rose up too. For the first and last time I hurled abuse at a Newcastle player. A stream of consciousness swear frenzy spewed out. The supporter in front of me had spun his head away in anguish and was clasping his hands to the side of his face like Munch's *The Scream*. He needed comforting, but copped my demented anger instead. Middle England celebrated as Man Utd did the double. I plunged into a trough of despair as first my double then my vindicative single vanished. I walked out of the ground a shattered man. I was sadder than the bus spotters cataloguing the coaches as they arrived at Wembley.

After a season of unmitigated angst I have taken the bold decision not to renew my season ticket. To do so would mean taking out another loan. Instead, my brother-in-law can use it. I'll have first call on any matches he can't make but otherwise I'll just wait until St James' Park can hold 50,000 then get to the games when I can. I'll become the perfect fan, that is, I won't be a fan at all, just a consumer.

This will be better both for myself and the club. No longer will I have to oppress and burden my family with childminding responsibilities. My daughter gets into Blyth and Bedlington for free, can run around to her heart's content and I can watch the match. In doing this I know I'll not have wasted my life either, because the game of football can be a joy and an inspiration. Conversely, I will have had a door opened to a path of purity, untainted by the wretched ambivalence forced upon me at St James' Park. I wouldn't have appreciated or even recognised this if I hadn't fallen out of love with Newcastle.

It's been a tough journey as I wrestled with my inner feelings and an even tougher decision for me to finally change course. Cowardice would have prevented me from making the leap but circumstances forced it upon me and now that I've done it I'm much happier.

But if a fan of my obsession, determination and durability cannot take any more then something must be wrong within the upper echelons. The people who run football should perhaps start to take notice.

contributors

Simon Bell comes from Guildford and works in publishing. His main hobby used to be mapping vantage points from which Woking's floodlights were visible. Happily, he has since married a kindly woman, has a son and lives in Brighton. He can't see the lights now, even using a ladder.

Ivan Briscoe has so far failed to meet Diego Maradona while working on the *Buenos Aires Herald*, but has heard the experience is bracing.

Rob Chapman is a freelance music writer for *Mojo* and a reviewer for the *Times*. Born in Bedford, he now lives in Stretford and his football allegiances have changed accordingly. He is old enough to remember crying when John White died.

John Earls, 27, was a glory-hunting Liverpool fan living in Milton Keynes until the age of nine, when he won a competition in the local paper to attend Luton's promotion-clinching game against Shrewsbury. After seeing Luton win 4-1 and having his photo taken with Brian Stein, he's been stuck with the Hatters ever since. A former journalist with the *Sunday People*, he is now a youth writer for Teletext.

Dave Espley is a computer programmer who has recently moved to a new job with Stockport Council, ostensibly for a large pay increase, but really because it's easier to get to Edgeley Park for cup tickets at lunchtime. He is married with three young potential fans.

Ken Gall is a founding member of the London Arabs, the capital's Dundee United supporters club. He works in a famous London institution known for its collection of chancers, time-servers and second-raters (not the FA though).

Harry Golightly's career path has seen him embrace the worlds of insurance, building sites, car valeting, record shops, bars, journalism, social work and, currently, film-making. His strongest ambitions are to produce the definitive football film, live in Leeds with "this very, very adorable girl" and raise a brood of tricky wingers who will play for Scunthorpe United for the duration of their careers.

Matthew Hall has watched and written about football in Italy, Croatia, Spain, France, Luxembourg, Mexico, New Zealand, the US, Australia, Wolverhampton and south London. He is currently writing *The Away Game*, the story of Australians playing in Europe.

Patrick Harverson is the sports correspondent of the *Financial Times*, where he writes about the news and business of sport. This means he covers football for four and a half days a week, leaving the final half day for all other sports. Having been born in Cyprus and brought up in Singapore, America and all over Britain, he is, inevitably, a Manchester United fan.

In 1966, Borussia Dortmund beat Liverpool in the final of the European Cup-Winners Cup. As the players paraded the trophy through the streets of Dortmund, **Ulrich Hesse-Lichtenberger** watched in amazement and vowed to erase life before football from his memory – a decision aided by the fact that he was not yet three months old.

Three decades later he is writing a book on the history of German football.

Neil Hurden is an occasionally bemused witness to the new-look Fulham. Genetically disposed to support the club, his first experience of seeing the dazzling feet of Les Barrett in action proved to be a dangerously enticing one. In his spare time he is a lawyer.

Steve James (Matt Nation) popped over to Hamburg for the weekend in 1990 and never came back. He thought FC St Pauli could occupy the Saturday afternoon slot previously filled by Bristol City, but they ruined it all by winning promotion in 1995.

Despite constant efforts to write less about football, **Simon Kuper** writes chiefly about football, prinicipally a column in the *Observer*. He is the author of *Football Against the Enemy*.

Justin McCurry was born in Wordsley in the west midlands in 1969. After graduating he ventured east for what was supposed to be a year of teaching and carefree travel, fully expecting Wolves to have been promoted by the time he returned. Eight years on, both have yet to make a move. He writes for the *Daily Yomiuri*.

Archie MacGregor is the former editor of and co-founder of the Scottish football fanzine *The Absolute Game* – currently in abeyance – and is now a freelance writer and broadcaster. Originally from Perth, he still wakes up in the middle of the night convinced last season never happened.

Davy Millar has endured several periods of employment in a variety of jobs but prefers to write as this doesn't necessitate getting out of bed. His articles on subjects other than football are regarded with suspicion by friends who see them as a futile attempt to mask his obsession with the game.

Gary Oliver, 37, is a regular contributor to *WSC* and the Raith Rovers fanzine *Stark's Bark* and by day masquerades as an accountant. He spent season 1998-99 campaigning for the removal of Raith manager Jimmy Nicholl (it happened) and urging that the breakaway Scottish Premier League be abolished (it wasn't).

The **Reverend Steve Parish** has been a Manchester City season ticket holder for nearly 30 years. Despite that, he still looks younger than he is. He missed an ordination service to go to Wembley last season, but Dickov's equaliser expiated any sense of guilt.

Piers Pennington was manager of the Intermediate Reds from 1994-97 and joint secretary of the Kingston Little League from 1996-99. His promiscuous devotion to Manchester City and Oxford United has enabled him to offer important advice to the next generation of footballers, the most valuable being "Never let them see you cry".

Ian Plenderleith is a freelance writer who has just been lured to Washington DC by the glamour and tradition of Major League Soccer. He is also an indie-pop Pop of two small girls, who will one day perhaps play for Lincoln City

Huw Richards is a freelance journalist who writes on rugby for the *Financial Times* and the *International Herald Tribune*. He lives in east London and, due to a genetic defect passed through the male line in his family, has supported Swansea since 1966. He is working with Huw Bowen on an oral history of the club.

Ken Sproat has traipsed around the football venues of Northumberland since birth and is now giving the same solid foundation for life to his daughter Bethan. He is a "pit yakka" by birth, an analyst programmer by trade and a cynical optimist by nature.

Mark Tallentire is a sub-editor on the *Guardian* sports desk. He watched his first Everton match, along with 49,000 others, in September 1969, a 2-0 (Ball, Husband) home win against West Ham.

Mike Ticher was a co-founder of *When Saturday Comes* and is now one of its editors. After deserting the magazine in 1988 he spent eight years living in Sydney, returning just in time to catch the end of a Chelsea era when David Lee was their idea of a cultured, ball-playing sweeper.

David Wangerin emigrated to Britain from Wisconsin in 1987 as part of Aston Villa's promotion push and has lived in the midlands ever since. For nine years he produced the obscure German football fanzine *Elfmeter* and in 1993 he compiled a statistical history of German football (copies of which, oddly enough, are still available). He is currently working on his first proper book.

Joyce Woolridge is a history lecturer and Manchester United fan. She began writing about football after Peter Osgood questioned her sobriety on a phone-in and is currently engaged in a PhD about professional footballers in postwar England.

BOOKS

WSC Books is a publishing imprint
created by the monthly independent
magazine *When Saturday Comes*, with the
aim of providing a platform for original
and innovative writing on football.
Always Next Year is the second new title to
appear under the imprint, following the
1998 World Cup book, *Back Home*.

We aim to publish a small number of
quality titles each year, which will address
topics outside the mainstream in an
intelligent and accessible manner.

We welcome ideas for book projects, and
draft manuscripts (please include an SAE).

WSC Books
3 Luke St
London
EC2A 4PX

also available...

Only £13.99 *UK*
Europe £15.99
Rest of World £19.99
All inc p+p

The First Eleven

The complete first 11 issues of *When Saturday Comes*. Long since out of print, the magazine's first outpourings recall a time when football was at its lowest ebb. This new edition (1998) includes a revised introduction and foreword by John Peel

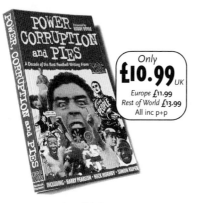

Only £10.99 *UK*
Europe £11.99
Rest of World £13.99
All inc p+p

Power, Corruption and Pies

Following on from where *The First Eleven* left off, this collection brings together the best writing from the next decade of *WSC*, 1988-97. Among the contributors are Harry Pearson, Nick Hornby, Simon Kuper and Dave Hill. The foreword is by Roddy Doyle

Only £10.99 *UK*
Europe £11.99
Rest of World £13.99
All inc p+p

Back Home

How The World Watched France 98
A collection of new writing which shifts the focus of the 1998 World Cup to the fans watching in the competing countries. Explains how David Batty unleashed mayhem in Buenos Aires mental hospitals and why you should always stay indoors in Sofia when Bulgaria lose

To order: Send your name, address, a cheque payable to *When Saturday Comes*, or your Visa/Mastercard details to:
***When Saturday Comes*, FREEPOST KE8091, London E2 8BR** (No Stamp Needed in UK*)
OR: CALL 24HR MASTERCARD/VISA LINE 0171 729 9461 FAX 0171 729 9417

If you are paying by credit card please enclose your credit card name, number, expiry date, and statement address if it is different to the one you wish your books to be delivered to. ***Overseas send to:** WSC, 17a Perseverance Works, 38 Kingsland Road, London E2 8DD, UK

THE HALF DECENT FOOTBALL MAGAZINE

WSC
When Saturday Comes

1 year subscription
£25.40 UK
Europe £32
Rest of World £39

When Saturday Comes is an independent monthly magazine focusing on all aspects of football culture from the fans' perspective. The magazine was started in 1986, a time when Luton Town were a force in the land and cabinet ministers were considerably less eager to identify themselves as football fans than they are now. *WSC* continues to produce critical football writing with a sense of humour. Look out for it underneath the pile of glossy football mags at your newsagents. Or, to be sure of securing a copy of the latest issue, visit Sportspages bookshop in London or Manchester.

Alternatively, take out a subscription to *WSC* and have your copy delivered to your door before it is in the shops. You'll be guaranteed the next 12 months of the best in independent football writing, plus any *WSC* supplements and freebies, all at an inflation-proof rate.

To order: Send your name, address, a cheque payable to *When Saturday Comes*, or your Visa/Mastercard details to:
When Saturday Comes, **FREEPOST KE8091, London E2 8BR** (No Stamp Needed in UK*)
OR: CALL 24HR MASTERCARD/VISA LINE 0171 729 9461 FAX 0171 729 9417

If you are paying by credit card please enclose your credit card name, number, expiry date, and statement address if it is different to the one you wish your books to be delivered to. *****Overseas send to:** *WSC*, 17a Perseverance Works, 38 Kingsland Road, London E2 8DD, UK